FILMMAKERS
On
FILMMAKING

Also Available from J. P. Tarcher, Inc.
FILMMAKERS ON FILMMAKING, Volume 1
edited by Joseph McBride

Hal Wallis, Studio Executive
Richard Zanuck and David Brown, Producers
Ingmar Bergman, Director
Billy Wilder and I.A.L. Diamond, Screenwriters
Sidney Poitier, Actor
Lucille Ball, Actress
James Wong Howe, Cinematographer
Leonard Rosenman, Composer
Polly Platt, Production Designer
Verna Fields, Editor
Anthea Sylbert, Costume Designer
Sue Mengers, Agent

Other Books by Joseph McBride

John Huston (editor)
Frank Capra (editor)
Hawks on Hawks
Astaire (editor)
High & Inside: The Complete Guide to Baseball Slang
Orson Welles: Actor and Director
Kirk Douglas
John Ford (with Michael Wilmington)
Focus on Howard Hawks (editor)
Orson Welles
Persistence of Vision (editor)

AMERICAN FILM INSTITUTE SEMINAR WITH CHARLTON HESTON.

FILMMAKERS
On
FILMMAKING

The American Film Institute
Seminars on Motion Pictures and Television

Edited by Joseph McBride

VOLUME TWO

J. P. TARCHER, INC.
Los Angeles
Distributed by Houghton Mifflin Company
Boston

Library of Congress Cataloging in Publication Data
Main entry under title:

Filmmakers on filmmaking.

Includes bibliographies.
1. Moving-pictures—Production and direction—Congresses.
2. Moving-picture acting—Congresses.—3. Moving-pictures—Setting
and scenery—Congresses. 4. Costume—Congresses. I. McBride,
Joseph. II. American Film Institute. III. Title: Filmmakers
on filmmaking.
PN1995.9.P7F5 1983   791.43   83-4722
ISBN 0-87477-267-2 (v. 2)
ISBN 0-87477-250-8 (pbk.: v. 2)

Design by Tanya Maiboroda

MANUFACTURED IN THE UNITED STATES OF AMERICA
V 10 9 8 7 6 5 4 3 2 1
First Edition

For Elaine

Contents

The best of film for me, and the worst of film, is that it is such a collaborative process. You are dealing with incredibly different kinds of people and, even worse than that, you are dependent upon incredibly different kinds of people. I pride myself on having specific conceptions of a film when I decide to do it, and a specific vision of what I want that film to be. But, unlike an author or a composer, I have now become dependent. I am working with a writer, I am working with the actors, I am working with a set designer, I am working with the cameraman, I am working with endless, endless numbers of people. It is enraging at times and it is also the most exciting part of it at times. In the end, if the film is successful, it is a synthesis of so many people that it is impossible to remember who did what and when.

Alan J. Pakula, director

Introduction

This book and its companion volume were drawn from more than a decade of lively discussion between Fellows of The American Film Institute and some of the world's most distinguished filmmakers. Many of the students who participated in the AFI seminars have since become prominent filmmakers themselves— among them, Terrence Malick, Paul Schrader, David Lynch, Amy Heckerling, Jeremy Paul Kagan, Tom Rickman, Matthew Robbins, and Caleb Deschanel—and what they have learned at the AFI has already enriched American film and television. The seminars are an invaluable part of the Fellows' education, an extraordinary opportunity to exchange ideas with masters of the art of filmmaking. To share that experience with the general public, these first two volumes of *Filmmakers on Filmmaking* have been assembled from the more than five hundred seminars held at the AFI since its inception.

The American Film Institute was established in 1967 by the National Endowment for the Arts as an independent, nonprofit national organization to advance the understanding and recognition of the moving image as an art form, to help preserve film and video for future generations, and to develop new talent. With the latter goal in mind, the Center for Advanced Film Studies was opened in Los Angeles in 1969 as a conservatory to teach aspiring filmmakers the basics of their art and craft. The AFI's founding director, George Stevens Jr., said at the dedication of the Center, "While it may not be possible to *train* people to make films, it is possible to create a climate in which people can *learn* to make films." The American professional filmmaking community and prominent visitors from around the world have given generously of their time and expertise to help create that climate of learning for a new generation of filmmakers.

The transcripts of the AFI seminars form a vast repository of oral history, a passing down of knowledge unrivaled in its scope since the beginning of the art form. As director Budd

1

Boetticher told the Fellows in 1970, "What a wonderful advantage it would have been had we had schools like you have here now, where people can ask questions. When I was twenty years old, I didn't get to walk up to John Ford and say, 'Tell me about your last picture.'" And, as cinematographer Howard Schwartz pointed out to the Fellows in 1973, "You don't realize how lucky you are that people want to explain to you how they do things. The whole atmosphere today is different. When I was an assistant cameraman, I had to sneak in on the conversations the director of photography had with his gaffer [chief electrician]. Everybody on the set was secretive. All of this wasn't available then."

Beyond their sheer informative value, the AFI seminars provide many vivid examples of the ways in which a professional filmmaker can share his or her experience for the enlightenment and inspiration of newcomers. Here we have Sidney Poitier telling the moving story of his early struggles to break down the walls preventing members of his race from equal status as filmmakers; Swedish director Ingmar Bergman communicating his joy in sharing the moment of creation with his actors; actress Lucille Ball describing her rise from chorus girl to head of a studio; screenwriter Robert Towne explaining how the clash of creative temperaments on *Chinatown* contributed to the complex mood of that modern film classic; producers Richard Zanuck and David Brown recalling the seemingly endless problems they faced on location for *Jaws*; legendary cinematographer James Wong Howe, after almost sixty years in the industry, retaining his youthful sense of wonderment as he eloquently discusses the nature of light; television producer Norman Lear describing his battles with network censors to bring controversial adult material to the home screen; and many more stories that take the reader inside the creative process of film and television with a rare degree of candor and insight.

If there is a common theme of these many and diverse seminars, it is that filmmaking, for better or worse, is an essentially collaborative process. There may be a dominant personality on or off the set, but even he or she must deal with the necessity of persuading several dozen people to work together for a common goal. While this point may seem an obvious one, it nevertheless has often been overlooked in the literature of film, which has tended to create personality cults around actors and directors at the expense of their less publicized but equally important collaborators such as screenwriters, producers, and cinematographers. *Filmmakers on Filmmaking* attempts to redress that imbalance by giving a comprehensive overview of the various functions involved in making a successful film.

Almost to an individual, the filmmakers who have given seminars at the AFI have been modest and grateful in acknowledging their debt to their fellow craftsmen. The Fellows have heard producer Joseph E. Levine stress that without a good script, no amount of money or effort can produce a good film; Charlton Heston explain the actor's need to depend on the taste and intelligence and skill of his "captain," the director; cinematographer John A. Alonzo give credit to an actor for helping establish the color scheme of a film; editor Verna Fields point out the contributions a musical composer can make to the pacing and emotion of a film; and Ingmar Bergman pay tribute to a producer who gave him the courage and the backing to survive a low point in his career. Throughout these books, filmmakers stress their interdependence with their co-workers and urge the Fellows to banish any thoughts of trying to be a one-man show.

But if filmmakers can also continue to support their claims to be considered artists as well as craftsmen, they must be able to continue finding means of self-expression within the commercial strictures of an impersonal industry; much time in AFI seminars is devoted to discussing that problem. So much, in fact, that Kirk Douglas kidded the Fellows during his 1975 seminar, "I thought I was going to be with a group of artists. All you want to talk about is money. I think you're getting near graduation time." But these concerns are rooted in the hard realities of professional filmmaking, which is, as Charlton Heston puts it, "the only art form in which the artist cannot afford to buy his own tools." The Center for Advanced Film Studies, AFI director Jean Firstenberg has written, teaches aspiring filmmakers the art and craft of their profession "while rooting that learning in the middle ground of the world of commerce. The balance inherent in this undertaking is crucial to the field, reflecting the balance between the work of the artist and the need of the craftsman to find his audience. It is a struggle that mankind has observed in all its art forms, but nowhere so clearly as with the moving image."

During most of the period covered in these volumes, seminars with distinguished guests were held on a weekly basis at the Center for Advanced Film Studies in the AFI's Greystone mansion in Beverly Hills, California; since 1981 the seminars have been held at the new AFI campus, the former Immaculate Heart College in Los Angeles. Each seminar was attended by an average of fifty to seventy-five Fellows, usually in an informal setting with the guest sitting on a couch surrounded by the Fellows. Three of each guest's most important films were screened during the days preceding the seminar so that Fellows would have fresh, specific, and well-informed questions. A few of the seminar transcripts were closed to the public at the request of the guests, but the great majority were inspected and approved by the guests before being made available for public access.

The first two volumes of *Filmmakers on Filmmaking* barely scratch the surface of the wealth of material available. I have been able to include only about 2 percent of the more than 5 million words (forty thousand pages) of transcripts in existence at the AFI's Louis B. Mayer Library on the new campus. This collection alone could provide material for an entire series of books, and the seminars are continuing on a regular basis each month at the Center for Advanced Film Studies.

Several factors governed the choice of seminars for these volumes. It was decided that the best way to reflect the true nature of the filmmaking process would be to include in each volume one representative seminar participant or team from each of several major filmmaking areas: studio executive, producer, director, screenwriter, actor, actress, cinematographer, composer, production designer, costume designer, and editor (although in the last category a second seminar of equal interest did not exist). Other seminars were drawn from such important contributors to films as the agent, the casting director, and the independent filmmaker. Only space limitations prevented the inclusion of seminars with other craftsmen who have shared their expertise with AFI Fellows, including stuntmen, special-effects creators, production managers, makeup artists, and songwriters, as well as seminars with such other figures as bankers, lawyers, laboratory technicians, story editors, publicists, journalists, and critics.

Nearly all of the seminar participants included in these volumes have been involved in an area or areas of filmmaking other than the one for which they are primarily known. It helps to underscore the hybrid nature of filmmaking that, for example, production designer Polly Platt is also a screenwriter; directors Ingmar Bergman, Jean Renoir, and Billy Wilder have also written their own films; Norman Lear, Joseph E. Levine, Richard Zanuck, and David Brown have been at various times both producers and studio executives; editor Verna Fields was also a studio executive; cinematographer John A. Alonzo began as an actor and later directed; Sidney Poitier has had successful careers as both actor and director; and so forth. Production designer Harry Horner, who has also directed, told the Fellows in 1976, "We all should know as much as possible about each other's specialties because, if nothing else, it widens the tolerance of one to the other. . . . The conductor could not work without the orchestra. The members are all on an equal level of importance."

Each of the seminars was considerably longer in transcript than in the edited form that appears here. An average AFI seminar lasts two or three hours and covers sixty or seventy pages of transcript, about three times as long as the average edited seminar in these volumes. To facilitate readability and to provide a clearer line of thought, I have in some instances rearranged material within a seminar (or from more than one seminar by a single participant) and clarified syntax, while still attempting to retain the flavor of conversational rather than written English. Occasional obvious mistakes and confusions of phrasing have been silently corrected, and explanatory background material has been added in brackets, but in no case has the sense of the speaker's words been changed by rewriting. I have, however, taken the liberty of rewriting some of the Fellows' questions to make them simpler, clearer, and more pointed.

As much as possible, I have tried to focus each seminar on topics of general application to the participant's field. Personal anecdotes that help to explain how a filmmaker does his or her particular job have been stressed more than anecdotes of an incidental nature, but care has also been taken to include stories that show how a participant became a filmmaker and how his or her individual artistic personality was formed.

I was faced with some difficult choices in selecting only twenty-four seminars from the more than five hundred available. In some cases it would have been possible to choose equally interesting seminars by other participants, and there the final balance was tipped by the general applicability of a seminar and by its success in relating the participant's craft to the other major filmmaking crafts. To give a taste of the richness of the other material available, some memorable and irresistible moments from other seminars are included in the back of each volume under the heading "Short Subjects."

While this is the first time that AFI seminars have been collected in a book, short versions of seminars have appeared monthly in the AFI's magazine, *American Film*, where portions of several of these seminars previously appeared. Some seminar material also appeared in the previous AFI books *Filmmaking: The Collaborative Art*, edited by Donald Chase, and *Directing the Film: Film Directors on Their Art*, edited by Eric Sherman. The complete seminar transcripts are available for reading by the public at the Louis B. Mayer Library on the campus in Los Angeles; some have also been converted to microfilm, and a few have been made available on videotape.

I wish to express appreciation to all the filmmakers who have given seminars at the AFI; to the AFI Fellows who have participated in them so enthusiastically; and to those people at the AFI most responsible for the ongoing success of the seminar program: AFI director Jean Firstenberg; founding director and current chairman of the Board of Trustees George Stevens Jr.; Center for Advanced Film Studies director Antonio Vellani; former AFI-West director Robert Blumofe; and, especially, the late James Powers, who was head of the seminar program from 1971 until his death in 1980 and conducted many of these seminars. Jim set a tone for the seminars that was both relaxed and serious-minded, and he laid the foundation without which these books could not exist.

Howard Schwartz, who conducts the highly knowledgeable cinematography seminars held by the AFI in conjunction with the American Society of Cinematographers, also deserves thanks, as does the keeper of the seminar transcripts, Anne G. Schlosser, director of the Louis B. Mayer Library. Library assistant Howard Prouty supplied useful information on seminar participants.

The most important assistance in the actual preparation of these books was given by the AFI's director of education services, Peter J. Bukalski, and his staff—Ann Martin, Ronald Mulligan, and Beth Wettergreen. Their patience, diligence, and advice were a constant source of encouragement and support. Jeanine Basinger, professor of film studies at Wesleyan University and a member of the AFI Board of Trustees, gave valuable guidance on the philosophy and content of the books. Eric Sherman and Robert A. Haller advised me on the Stan Brakhage seminar. And, finally, the intelligent and sympathetic editorial contributions of Janice Gallagher and copy editor Georgia Griggs were crucial factors in making these volumes a pleasurable experience.

Los Angeles
February 1983

Joseph McBride

Norman Lear

"A humorous spotlight on our frailties, prejudices, and concerns" was the description offered to audiences of the first television series produced by Norman Lear, *All in the Family,* and those words characterize all of his subsequent work in the medium. As a producer and executive during the 1970s, Lear became the single most influential creative force in American entertainment.

Through his independent companies in partnership with Bud Yorkin and later Jerry Perenchio—Tandem Productions, TAT Communications, and Embassy Communications—Lear successfully challenged the entrenched myth that the average TV viewer has the mental capacity of a child. He introduced controversial adult themes, strong language, and true-to-life characters in his precedent-shattering 1971 series *All in the Family* and followed it with hit after hit: *Sanford & Son*; *Maude*; *Good Times*; *The Jeffersons*; *One Day at a Time*; *Mary Hartman, Mary Hartman*; *Diff'rent Strokes*; *The Facts of Life*; and *Archie Bunker's Place*.

Born in Connecticut in 1922, Lear was a publicist before moving to Los Angeles, where he worked as a door-to-door salesman and a sidewalk photographer. He formed a writing partnership with Ed Simmons to sell jokes and song parodies to nightclub performers. In 1950, David Susskind, then an agent and later a prominent producer, found them a job writing a TV variety show, *The Ford Star Revue*.

They then wrote the highly popular Dean Martin and Jerry Lewis *Colgate Comedy Hour* and *The Martha Raye Show* (which Lear also directed). On his own, Lear wrote Tennessee Ernie Ford's show and wrote and directed *The George Gobel Show*. He joined with director Yorkin in 1959 to form Tandem, which made specials featuring such stars as Fred Astaire, Danny Kaye, Jack Benny, Carol Channing, and Henry Fonda. They branched into features in 1963 with *Come Blow Your Horn* and made six other films, including *Cold Turkey*, which Lear directed in 1971.

Returning to TV on the advice of their business manager, Tandem took a BBC-TV series about a working-class bigot, *Till Death Do Us Part*, and transformed it into *All in the Family*, with Carroll O'Connor as Archie Bunker. The controversial CBS-TV show became the most popular comedy series ever presented on television. Another British series, *Steptoe & Son*, provided the basis for Tandem's second hit, *Sanford & Son*, with Redd Foxx.

A crusader for liberal causes both on-screen and off, Lear helped promote minority hiring in television and has been active in the American Civil Liberties Union. In 1981, angered at the censorship tactics of the Moral Majority, he helped form People for the American Way and later produced a patriotic special, *I Love Liberty*.

Lear stepped away from the day-to-day operations of his companies' series in 1978. Since 1977 he has been active in cable TV systems, and he returned to filmmaking in 1982 when he and Perenchio used their TV profits to purchase Avco Embassy Pictures, which they renamed Embassy Pictures.

FILMOGRAPHY

1963 *Come Blow Your Horn* (writer, producer)   1965 *Never Too Late* (producer)   1967 *Divorce, American Style* (writer)   1968 *The Night They Raided Minsky's* (writer, producer)   1971 *Start the Revolution Without Me* (executive producer) / *Cold*

Turkey (writer, producer, director) 1974 *The Thief Who Came to Dinner* (production executive) 1978 *Blue Collar* (production executive)

TELEVISION SERIES
(as producer and/or production executive;
original air dates listed)

1971–79 *All in the Family* 1972–77 *Sanford & Son* 1972–78 *Maude* 1974–79 *Good Times* 1975 *Hot l Baltimore* 1975— *The Jeffersons* / *One Day at a Time* 1976 *The Dumplings* / *The Nancy Walker Show* 1976–77 *All's Fair* 1976–78 *Mary Hartman, Mary Hartman* 1977 *All That Glitters* / *Fernwood 2Night* / *A Year at the Top* / *The Sanford Arms* / *Forever Fernwood* 1978 *America 2Night* / *Apple Pie* 1978–79 *In the Beginning* 1978 *Diff'rent Strokes* 1979 *Highcliffe Manor* / *Hangin' In* / *The Baxters* / *Joe's World* 1979–80 *Hello, Larry* 1979 *The Facts of Life* / *Archie Bunker's Place* 1980–81 *Sanford* / *Palmerstown, U.S.A.* (aka *Palmerstown*) 1982— *Gloria* / *Silver Spoons* / *Square Pegs*

THE SEMINAR

Norman Lear held a seminar with the Fellows of the Center for Advanced Film Studies on February 28, 1977.

You've maintained a strong control over the quality and the social responsibility of your shows. How do you organize your production staff so that as the volume of your output increases you don't lose control of the principles you have come to represent on television?

LEAR: No one person can do everything when a company gets past a certain size. We've become a very homogeneous group of people in the sense that we wish to do the same kind of theater— theater of content. We don't mind if we do three minutes without a laugh. By the same token, we don't mind if a scene is hilarious without content. But we are not homogeneous in the sense of sharing the same ideas; that's why, I hope, there's a richness in the tapestry.

I'm involved in all of the shows where either an individual episode requires me or the theme compels my involvement. A couple of weeks may go by on any of the shows when I'm not around much, but I'm involved in the scripts because I love that. Other people develop a script, and when they get it to a certain place, they will call me in to ask what I think. But there's no way we can have me totally involved in developing shows and do the shows that are on the air at the same time.

I worked infinitely harder when I used to write one screenplay than I do now. I used to kill myself on a screenplay. First I'd sit for two months picking my head, which is why I wear a silly-looking hat. My wife bought me that to keep me from picking my head. Then I would sit for the next two months asking myself, "My God, where would you be if you hadn't picked your head for two months?" I'd eat my heart out until ten or eleven at night or two in the morning. I'd cancel dinner engagements, and I'd miss time on weekends with my kids. I'd finally write the screenplay in three or four weeks at the very end, sometimes living at the studio, working around the clock. I remember a New Year's Eve when my wife and friends came to see me shortly after midnight with paper hats and party favors. All over one bloody screenplay.

In your early years as a television writer with Dean Martin and Jerry Lewis, did you learn any lessons that carry over into your work today?

LEAR: Everything is a learning experience. Ed Simmons and I wrote the first three years of the Martin and Lewis part of *The Colgate Comedy Hour,* and as crazy as those sketches and stand-up segments were, I always thought we were saying something. I thought of Jerry Lewis as a kind of Everyman. Dean and Jerry became the toast of the nation practically overnight, and we were all big heroes off those shows. But I remember going to a Chinese restaurant with my agent the night after the third show; I spent the evening weeping because I thought Jerry had screwed up something we were saying. That's a long way of saying I learned a great deal from Dean and Jerry.

One thing occurs to me that I'd love to tell you, those of you who write. I was twenty-seven when I started with Martin and Lewis. I was married and had a child, and I could afford to die because I had insurance, but I couldn't afford to be ill for any length of time. That used to worry me. Then one day in my thirties I realized that, because I was a writer, as long as I could talk and had a brain I would be able not only to support myself but to create roles that would enable other people to work, too. That's the greatest security in the world: knowing you can do something that can hardly be taken away from you.

How did I get so serious so fast? You're all so serious-looking—I think you're doing it to me. I like it, but I didn't expect to be serious so soon.

How did you get your first break as a writer?

LEAR: I was lucky. I came out here when I was twenty-six. I had been through World War II and I had been a press agent for a couple of years. Then I met Ed Simmons, and one night we wrote a song parody we liked and we sold it to a nightclub singer for $25. In a couple of hours I had made a dollar more than I had made that whole day at another job [during that period Lear worked as a sidewalk photographer and a door-to-door furniture salesman]. So we took a little office above a delicatessen—it cost $5 a month, that's how little it was—and we wrote every night. We'd run out to nightclubs and sell these things for $25 or $30. Gradually that began to be more important than the money we were making during the day.

One afternoon I had an idea for a routine for Danny Thomas, so I called his agent's office. In the army when I was picked up by the MPs I always used the name "Merle Robinson," who was a friend of mine as a kid, so I said, "I am Merle Robinson. I'm with the *New York Times*. I'm at the airport and I'm ready to leave. I've been here for two days interviewing Danny Thomas, and there's a terribly important question I haven't asked him." They gave me his number immediately. I called him, and he was with his pianist getting ready to do a Friars' Frolic [an evening of entertainment held by the Los Angeles branch of the Friars Club, a show-business fraternal organization] three nights later. Hé was fascinated with the way I had gotten his number; it made him laugh. I said, "I've got a routine for you. It's three stories about three Yiddish words and what they mean—*shammes* [sexton], *tummel* [commotion], and *farblondjet* [mixed up]." He said, "Can you get it here in half an hour?" I said I couldn't, because I hadn't written it. This was around three in the afternoon. I showed up at six with the material. He paid me $500 and did it three nights later. David Susskind, who was an agent at that time, asked him who wrote it, and then called me to ask if I'd ever done television. I said, "Of course." On the plane to New York I studied television scripts, and I got off the plane and, with Ed Simmons, started writing a weekly one-hour show called *The Ford Star Revue*.

Fred Friendly says in his book Due to Circumstances Beyond Our Control *that as long as television is based on a mercantile system it's never going to be able to delve into subject matter of any great importance. How would you respond to that?*

LEAR: Television can do whatever people in television want to do. Granted we do comedy, and granted we're limited to half an hour, but we just did two episodes on lung cancer on *Good Times*, and on *Maude* last week Nanette Fabray played an old friend of Maude's who had suffered a stroke. Over the Christmas holidays we had amnesty for Vietnam War resisters on *All in the Family*. We deal with subjects that matter to me.

But you deal with them in a comedy format.

LEAR: So did a lot of our predecessors. The history of literature and the theater is rife with important subject matter dealt with in a comedic vein.

What do you think of the movie Network *[written by Paddy Chayevsky, directed by Sidney Lumet, 1976]? The ads claimed, "After this, television will never be the same," but I think television is immune to this kind of analysis.*

LEAR: I don't think Paddy Chayevsky was talking only about television; he was talking about what the world and this country have become in terms of sacrificing all human values and all esthetics to the business of profit. The great Ned Beatty speech toward the end of the picture was hardly about television. It was about what is ruling the world.

How do you account for the fact that television is not more concerned with looking at itself as an institution and as an art form?

LEAR: Television doesn't have to be concerned with looking at itself. Everybody else is doing that. Nobody knows what your dentist is doing in your mouth, and we don't know what General Motors is going to do to us this year on the highway, but we all know what's happening on television. The *Los Angeles Times* and most other major metropolitan dailies week in and week out print the ratings of the top ten shows, the bottom ten shows, the network that's ahead by such-and-such a fraction of a percentage. There's too much written about television.

I got a call today from *TV Guide*: "How do you feel about *All in the Family* being number thirteen last week?" They were looking for bitterness. I'm supposed to be terribly unhappy that in its sixth year *All in the Family* has fallen so far out of grace that it is number thirteen. How do I tell the man that the kick in doing the show was always in doing the individual episodes, when we either knocked out the audience with something wonderful or we blew it.

And yet the business is all based on ratings, winning and losing. That seems to be the problem. Who are the people who really decide what's going to be on TV?

LEAR: The presidents of ABC, CBS, and NBC; a handful of people who help them; and the research groups. They'll take a pilot a company does and give it to a couple of research firms called ASI and the Audience Research Institute. What they do is show it to, let's say, a hundred "average viewers." Well, my idea of average viewers is the millions of people sitting at home in their shirt-sleeves watching television. Calling a hundred people off the streets and putting little straps on their arms to measure their pulses—telling them, "Dial this if you like it, dial this if you don't like it," and then asking them forty minutes of questions afterward and taping it—that's hardly asking an average viewer. Something must happen to an individual that turns him from an average viewer into something else the minute he's treated this way.

I wonder about polling. Polling is supposed to result in such sure knowledge. When they researched *All in the Family* the people laughed because it was funny. But when they were asked if they would like it on the air every week, they said no, because the man was a bigot and was saying terrible things. People often answer the way they think you'd like them to answer and keep their feelings to themselves.

Do you believe you can teach people something with a show such as Mary Hartman, Mary Hartman?

LEAR: No, I don't really think so. But there are things we do that are measurable, especially on health issues. We found by checking with the American Heart Association how many black males went for checkups within the week following the broadcast of an episode about hypertension on *Good Times*. We're so well connected with health institutions across the country that we let them know in advance when a show is coming up that has a health orientation, and we get the feedback immediately.

I met with Nicholas Johnson [then the chairman of the Federal Communications Commission] just before I came here, and he told me that the producer of one of the police shows had asked the star to fasten his seat belt every time he got into his car. In three weeks there was an enormous increase in the use of seat belts and the purchase of seat belts. So there are certain things you can measure quickly, but attitudinally I don't really know what changes.

Does that mean murders increase every time a murder is shown on TV?

LEAR: I don't think so. I think fastening a seat belt is easier for the average individual than murder. I could be wrong.

Could you explain how the characters in your comedies evolve?

For instance, how Edith Bunker [played by Jean Stapleton] began on All in the Family *and how she's changed.*

LEAR: Edith has been caught up in the women's movement, which caught all of us, our awareness, our consciousness. We provide Edith with her thoughts, her words, and her attitudes, and as we grow as people and as artists, and as times change, the characters reflect that.

Is that change a combination of the writer, the director, and the actor or actress?

LEAR: Ours is a giant collaboration. Scripts may be rewritten three or four or five times before actors see them, and when actors see them they may be redone again. Pieces may be redone daily because they're having problems in rehearsal. Then after three days of rehearsal there is a run-through, followed by one to four hours of heavy work on the script, making cuts, additions, whatever. The next morning there is a brand-new script out of mimeo and everybody is rehearsing on camera. At the end of that day there is a camera run-through, because some of the things in the rehearsal hall play differently on camera. Changes are made again in a session that may take several hours. The next day they're on camera for taping. There's a five-thirty taping and a note session, then an eight o'clock taping. We may make some mistakes in the tapings, so we'll do an hour's worth of pickup shots after that. In that whole process the actor is heard from a great deal, the director is heard from a great deal, and the writers are heard from again and again.

How do you work with the writers, say in developing a character such as Mary Hartman?

LEAR: *Mary Hartman* was a concept I had many years ago. I wanted to do an ongoing show that didn't have to have a beginning, middle, and end every day. I wanted stories that would grip a mass audience and would also be off-the-wall and satiric enough to grip a smaller audience. I always thought that I wasn't patronizing the American public and that lots of other people in television were, but I really was being patronizing when I thought that way, because I've learned that people who are gripped by the stories also understand the comedy. The people who understand the comedy are not so damned special. People are people.

I had five scripts done at that time. I wrote a couple; other writers wrote the others. ABC, which had put up development money, didn't want to go ahead with it. Then years later I thought I would try it again. I started talking to writers. I told them I wanted a mass murder to happen in the first week—a family around the block is killed, including eight chickens and two goats. Writer after writer said, "There's no way that can be funny." And I said, "It *isn't* funny. People's *reactions* to it are funny." It is sadly funny that people watch people being napalmed in Vietnam on the six o'clock news, and the next moment they go to their refrigerator for a beer. Finally, after about forty writers, Gail Parent said, "I understand." We worked out storylines and characters, including Mary Hartman. I cast Louise Lasser, and Joan Darling came to it as director. *Mary Hartman* would not have been the same had another actress played the character, and it probably would not have been the same if another director had directed it. All of those components were important.

How did you succeed in bypassing the networks with Mary Hartman *and selling it directly to independent stations?*

LEAR: The networks would not buy *Mary Hartman*. [CBS financed the making of two pilot episodes but decided not to air them.] And the *Wall Street Journal* did an article about it: "The Show That Three Networks Turned Down." That started independent stations calling and asking about it, because all the stations are looking for new independent programming, instead of just old reruns, to counter the network programming. I invited about thirty-five people from around the country who represented maybe seventy-five or eighty stations to my house for dinner.

They found that I have a wife and two daughters, that I am a respectable citizen and not a flaming radical, which the networks had told them I was. Nor was I a head-in-the-clouds, crazy artist, which the networks also told them I was. And they were not tight-assed conservatives who wouldn't buy anything, as the networks had told me they were. We found out that we were all human beings, and that was very important.

The next morning they looked at two episodes, which was all we had of *Mary Hartman*. Al Flanagan, a fellow who owned five stations—who I had been told was the most conservative, a guy who hated me and would hate the show—threw up his hand as soon as the episodes ended and said, "I want that for my stations. You name the price." He stunned all the others, and that started the ball rolling. Most of them bought it without understanding what they had watched. They just needed product so badly and hoped.

When you first pitched Mary Hartman *to the networks, did you really expect they would break their pattern in prime time and put on five shows a week?*

LEAR: The second year three networks wanted to. They begged us.

Why wouldn't you let them?

LEAR: Because we were very happy doing it the way we were doing it, and we didn't want to disappoint the independent stations who were, for the first time, able to fight the networks. It was fun helping them with that. [In 1980, four years after *Mary Hartman* premiered on the independent stations, CBS aired late-night reruns of the series.]

Had you ever considered syndicating a show in that way before? Before that there was a prevailing economic theory that a production company couldn't profitably handle syndication itself.

LEAR: I didn't know anything or think about syndication until *Mary Hartman* was lying fallow. Economic theories exist until somebody breaks them. It's not a loser's business any longer. *Mary Hartman* lost money when we started, because it was a buyer's market. Only a couple of them understood what they were buying, so we played a game that's often played in this business: we convinced ourselves that we could make it for the money we sold it for. This year *Mary Hartman* will pay for what it lost last year and will be profitable—infinitely more profitable for the stations than it will be for us. The fact is that television is an absolute license to print money for the average independent station. Next time we'll know a little more.

In network television, you do a show like *Maude* or *All in the Family*, and the network buys the show for the smallest dollar it possibly can. They don't know whether it's going to be successful, and you can't promise them it will be. If it dies, it's off the air in six weeks and nobody is angry at anybody. But if it becomes a smash, everybody becomes instant enemies. The actor, who deserves more money, says, "I want it." We say to the network, "He deserves more money. She deserves more money. We want to get it for them. And *we* deserve more money—we delivered you a hit." The network says, "Screw you. You've got a contract." So the way television is structured, at the moment when everybody should be breaking out a bottle of champagne, that's the moment they become enemies.

Did you deficit-finance All in the Family *or any of your other network shows [that is, produce them for more than the network licensing fee in hopes of future profits from syndication]?*

LEAR: No, we're on tape, and one of the happy things about tape is that the amount of money we could lose would be very modest. The post-production problems on tape are not the same as they are for film, so we break even, make a little money or lose a little, but we don't have important deficits.

The four-camera tape technique with a live audience is the one that excites me most. I love live audiences. I like the idea that you can't cheat. You can't bring somebody through a door and have him say, "Hello, darling, I'm home," and have a machine laugh. Either the audience laughs or it doesn't, and you have to write better that way.

Do any stations decide not to air certain Mary Hartman *episodes that contain material they don't like?*

LEAR: We said "God damn it" once and lost a station. Pat Gimble [the character played by Susan Browning], who is the subject of wife abuse, was yelling at her husband and said "God damn it." And I recall hearing that something was excised someplace; I would quarrel with that, but it is their right. But I can't remember hearing that an episode wasn't run.

Would you rather deal with those problems yourself than fight a network over censorship?

LEAR: I like it this way. I like the idea that there is no Program Practices Department looking over my shoulder. I like the fact that I don't have to have silly arguments.

This year on *Good Times*, the grandfather came to visit and brought a woman with him. Everybody assumed they had gotten married, so they were given a bedroom. Then the family learned that they weren't married. Florida [the mother, played by Esther Rolle] said, "You mean to tell me that you're . . . ," and the thirteen-year-old [Ralph Carter] supplied what she was looking for: "Shacking up?" It got a very warm, dear laugh. But five days earlier the network had said, "You can't do that." We said, "We think it'll be all right." Finally they told us they would let the kid say "getting it on." We couldn't believe it—they'll let us say "getting it on" but not "shacking up"?

It got to the point where, two nights before the broadcast, the network wanted us to tape him saying "getting it on" just in case we liked it better. I knew that would be a trap—if they had it, they would use it. But they were ready to excise the line, and I told the head of the department in New York, "If it's on the air without that moment I'm not going to be here tomorrow or any other day." Their threat is always lawsuits and so forth, and my response is, "Back up the truck, take the house and the furniture. I know the law prevents you from taking the kids."

You have tackled a lot of sensitive areas in your shows, but one thing bothers me. Part of a recent episode of All in the Family *took place in a synagogue, and it seems that in your shows, as much as on any other shows, anyone who is Jewish is a sixty-year-old bald man with a pot belly and a European accent. Do you ever plan to have a Jewish character who is not a stereotype?*

LEAR: There have been young Jews on *All in the Family* quite a number of times. There was a memorable show in which a swastika was painted on Archie's door and a young member of the Jewish Defense League came to defend what he was sure was a Jewish household. The argument grew from whether "an eye for an eye" or a pacifist attitude was right, and at the end of the show the JDL guy walked out still defending his position, stepped on a bomb starter, and was blown to bits. Sammy Davis Jr. has been on *All in the Family*, and he was also under sixty and Jewish. There were others.

You mentioned earlier that Mary Hartman *would have been different if a different director had directed it. How do you go about choosing a director?*

LEAR: Instinct. With somebody who hasn't done it before, that's all you can go by. Kim Friedman came to *Mary Hartman* from the AFI and from the theater, with the New York producer Joe Papp. She had not directed television before, but I didn't think it would be a problem for her. If she watched us work for a couple of weeks and said she could do it, my bet was that she could, and that's how it worked.

Why do you change directors so much on Mary Hartman?

LEAR: Because it's very hard, and after a few weeks they're exhausted. We do a show a day; we rehearse in the morning and tape in the afternoon. Nessa Hyams Picker, a graduate of the AFI Directing Workshop for Women, started again today. She's been off for four weeks; now she'll work three or four and then be replaced by Kim. Then she'll come back.

Is this strictly a woman-director assignment?

LEAR: No, Jim Drake has been the woman directing the last two weeks.

Allan Manings [executive producer of Good Times*] told us that due to your instigation* Good Times *had started a black writers' open-door policy. He said they had received about ten thousand scripts but hadn't found any that were good enough to make. Are you seriously looking for black writers?*

LEAR: Yes, of course we are. There *are* black writers on *Good Times*, though perhaps not as many as there ought to be. But there aren't as many good black writers in California as there ought to be, either, and that's because the door has been open for only a little while. Most of the people who are writing TV shows have been doing what they're doing for twenty or more years. There are no black writers with long lists of credits on television. But there are probably more *young* black writers working in our company than there are young white writers, in an attempt to rectify the situation. In a few years that's all going to be over. There are a lot of new writers starting.

What about directors? There are only a handful of black directors in television.

LEAR: Well, it's hard. We have an open-door policy for directors. We have invited or been asked by dozens of people—black and white, mostly white, because not that many blacks have asked—to observe the taping in the rehearsal schedule. I don't mean to be the least bit discouraging, but to someone who didn't grow up either behind a camera or on a stage, there's something very intimidating about calling shots on four cameras with a live audience and cutting it as you're going along, with the rhythm changing because the audience is laughing where you didn't think they'd laugh. It intimidated *me* years ago. I directed the actors and somebody else did the cameras. In all the years people have observed our tapings I've had only two people say, "I would like to try it," and both of them failed.

Were they black?

LEAR: Yes. But Gerren Keith is black, and he's directing *Good Times*. He grew up in it, you see; he was a stage manager and a cameraman.

Taking that into consideration, how can you make your living in an art when you find it difficult even to sneak past the guard at the gate?

LEAR: It's hard. I know it's hard. I don't know what to tell you. If I wanted to direct and had no other place, I'd be in a storefront someplace or in a loft working with seven actors day in and day out and learning how to communicate with them and Ibsen. You'd be amazed how many people come in and tell me "I'm ready to direct," but after talking to them for fifteen minutes you know that man or that woman may know a lot about the camera but is not going to be able to deal with actors. It does take a certain amount of living and knowledge and experience to deal with actors, to know how to move them and talk to them and deal with their problems as human beings and as the characters they're playing.

But then the problem is, how do you get your foot in the door?

LEAR: Well, look what I did. I told you how I got Danny Thomas on the phone. It wasn't by any usual method. Look what Sylvester Stallone did. He wrote a screenplay for himself—*Rocky*; Jimmy Caan wanted to play it; Stallone turned down everybody and insisted he would play it, and he finally found a couple of people [producers Robert Chartoff and Irwin Winkler] who believed in him, and he played it. Anybody who is going to break into any of these areas is not going to do it in a conventional way.

Are you ever going back to making movies?

LEAR: I'm dying to do it again. [Lear returned to movies in 1982 when he and Jerry Perenchio bought Avco Embassy Pictures.] The film I directed, *Cold Turkey*, was the greatest experience of my life. The difference with film is that you can really make love to a film, and you can't do that with television. On television you see things you want to do so badly you could kill, but you have to let them go because the damn clock is running. But the exciting thing about television is that if you have a good idea and something to say, you can have it on the air in five weeks and 40 million people see it. That's exciting as hell.

Joseph E. Levine

To quote from his official biography (1979), "For the last forty-five years, Joseph E. Levine has towered above lesser moguls of filmdom like a short, bespectacled colossus, making legends, making myths, making instant millions." This brand of bravura showmanship is characteristic of Levine, who has produced or presented nearly five hundred films.

Unabashedly straddling the twin poles of art and exploitation, Levine made his first impact as a distributor of such 1940s Italian masterpieces as *Open City, Paisan,* and *The Bicycle Thief,* but became known as a "promotional genius" in the 1950s for his handling of the camp classics *Godzilla* and *Hercules.* With his continued importing of foreign hits and his own production of *The Graduate* in 1967, Levine built his Embassy Pictures into a major industry force before relinquishing control and returning to one-man operation with Joseph E. Levine Presents, Inc.

Born in Boston in 1905, he grew up in poverty, quitting school at age fourteen to work in a garment factory. His later occupations included ambulance driver, dress shop owner, and restaurateur. In 1938 he purchased his first theater, an art house in New

Haven, Connecticut. The first two films he exhibited uncannily presaged his later career: one was the French classic *Un Carnet du Bal*, the other a cheapie two-reeler entitled *How to Undress in Front of Your Husband*.

During the 1940s Levine acquired several more theaters and began distributing foreign films in New England. But he decided he could not live by art alone, so in 1956 he purchased the American rights to the Japanese monster movie *Godzilla* for $12,000 and promoted it into a hit. In 1959 he stunned the industry with his unprecedented national saturation-booking campaign for the Italian "sword and sandal" epic *Hercules*, starring Steve Reeves. The film, which opened simultaneously in six hundred theaters, grossed about $5 million, quadrupling Levine's investment. Saturation booking has since become a common distribution process.

Levine's Embassy Pictures was highly active in international filmmaking during the 1960s, co-producing, financing, or distributing such foreign hits as *8½*, *Two Women*, *Darling*, *Romeo and Juliet*, and *Divorce, Italian Style*. In that same period Levine first ventured into domestic production with such films as *The Carpetbaggers*, *Nevada Smith*, *The Producers*, and *The Graduate*.

In 1968 he sold his company to the Avco Corporation, but remained chief executive officer of the renamed Avco Embassy. Although he was involved with such rewarding films as *The Lion in Winter* (his personal favorite among his productions) and *Carnal Knowledge*, Levine found the arrangement with Avco restrictive and resigned in 1974.

Since then his independent company has acquired foreign films, including *The Night Porter*, and has produced *A Bridge Too Far*, *Magic*, *. . . And Justice for All*, and *Tattoo*. He is a former member of the AFI Board of Trustees.

SELECTED FILMOGRAPHY
(as distributor, production executive, or producer)

1945 *Open City* 1946 *Paisan* 1948 *The Bicycle Thief* 1956 *Godzilla* 1959 *Hercules* 1961 *Two Women / Divorce, Italian Style / The Sky Above, The Mud Below* 1962 *Boccaccio '70* 1963 *8½ / Yesterday, Today, and Tomorrow* 1964 *Zulu / The*

Carpetbaggers / *Where Love Has Gone* / *Marriage, Italian Style*
1965 *Darling* / *Harlow* (Carroll Baker version) / *The Tenth
Victim* / *Sands of Kalahari* 1966 *Nevada Smith* / *The Oscar*
1967 *The Graduate* / *The Producers* / *Woman Times Seven*
1968 *The Lion in Winter* / *Romeo and Juliet* 1969 *Sun-
flower* / *Don't Drink the Water* 1970 *Soldier Blue* 1971 *Carnal Knowledge* 1972 *A Touch of Class* 1973 *The Day of the
Dolphin* 1974 *The Night Porter* 1977 *A Bridge Too Far*
1978 *Magic* 1979 . . . *And Justice for All* 1980 *Tattoo*

THE SEMINAR

Joseph E. Levine held a seminar with the Fellows of the Center for Advanced Film Studies on April 26, 1979.

What do you look for when you make a picture? You've made such a diversity of films. We've shown A Bridge Too Far, Magic, *and* The Graduate.

LEVINE: Well, with *The Graduate,* I met [director] Mike Nichols nine or ten years ago when he was doing *The Knack* in a theater I owned off-Broadway. I watched him rehearse. He was a genius of Broadway then and still is. I said, "Why don't you make a movie?" The next day he brought in the book *The Graduate* by Charles Webb, and I read it. He asked, "How'd you like it?" I said it was the worst thing I'd ever read in my life. "Then you won't make it?" I said, "I'll make it if *you* want to make it."

So in that case you went on his judgment?

LEVINE: I do that often. *The Lion in Winter* is a case in point. That was a case where I *did* like the script, which was based on a play by James Goldman. We were having a breakfast meeting in London; we were nine days away from shooting a film called *The Ski Bum.* We were supposed to be all ready, but the director, Anatole Litvak, said, "I must tell you, Joe, that this is the worst script I have ever read in my life." I was stunned; without the script, of course, you can't have a good movie.

   Peter O'Toole was supposed to star in it, to play the part of a Jewish ski bum. I desperately wanted him to do something for me—we were good friends—and he agreed to do this very bad picture. I said, "Why are you doing it if it's so bad?" He said, "I need the money." Which, as you probably have learned, is not a nice thing to do. At the same time I was making *The Graduate* and *The Producers,* and I was in trouble because *The Ski Bum* was budgeted for $4 million, money was committed to the crew, and $750,000 to Peter O'Toole, pay or play. So if we canceled the picture, we'd have to pay him.

   Now, I had read the script of *The Lion in Winter* several weeks before this meeting. I wanted to make it but there was no way to do it; the funds were kind of low then. But when this happened, I got hold of Martin Poll, a producer who owned the script, and made a deal with him the same day. Then I woke up Peter O'Toole, who had read the script; everybody had read *The Lion in Winter*, but nobody wanted to do it. But I liked it and Peter liked it. Before the weekend was over, I signed the papers with Poll, bought the script, hired Katharine Hepburn, hired Peter, and switched pictures, which I don't believe had ever been done before. In three months we were shooting. The picture came in on schedule, but it did not win the Academy Award [for best picture; it did win an Oscar for Hepburn as best actress].

With Dustin Hoffman in The Graduate, *you and Mike Nichols started a new trend in movie stars by making a lead out of an actor who wasn't classically handsome.*

LEVINE: That's what Mike was looking for—somebody who didn't look like a movie star. Dustin Hoffman was working for me at the time on an off-Broadway play, Arthur Miller's *A View from the Bridge*, as the stage manager. Mike brought him into my office in the Time-Life Building. It had been raining and the windows leaked, and when Dusty came in with a towel on his head I thought he was the plumber to fix the leaks. He was a delightful young man in those days.

How did Carnal Knowledge *come about?*

LEVINE: After *The Graduate* Mike said to me, "I want to make a funny dirty picture." And he did. After that, we had two scripts we were considering. One was a picture about a rabbi, and the other was *The Day of the Dolphin*. We took a long time before we decided whether we should make, with no disrespect, the Jew picture or the fish picture. Unfortunately, we chose the fish picture. I thought it was great when we were making it, and even when I saw it finished, but it just didn't work. Even when you have a picture like that, you're able to get advances and sell the television rights, so we came out whole. All we left behind was Mike's dignity.

What do you think of market analysis?

LEVINE: If you stop to analyze a picture, with all these guys sitting around at a board of directors' meeting and they don't want to make it because the wind is coming from the southeast—I mean, that's a lot of bunk. If you want to make it, *make* it. Many of the decisions I've made I've made quickly. *The Graduate* is the most successful film I ever made. That book had been to every film company in Hollywood. The author was lucky that he found Mike Nichols. Mike Nichols was lucky that he found me. But, you know, I hear a lot of talk about luck, and it irritates me. It's not luck at all. It's a lot of hard work.

What we're trying to find out from you is whether there is a central element that you look for in a film project.

LEVINE: I think he [the initial questioner] answered it by saying that I have not stuck with any type of film. Many years ago all I did was make and buy and produce and co-produce the films that came out of Italy and France, the so-called "art pictures." I found that if I stuck to that business I would soon be a shoemaker or a butcher. A lot of people think I should have been. At that time, way back in the days of *Open City* and *Paisan* [Italian films directed by Roberto Rossellini, 1945 and 1946]—I didn't make those, I just distributed them—there were only two hundred and fifty theaters in the United States where you could play an art film. It wasn't enough to break even on the picture. So I had to make other pictures, which got me into the commercial end of the business. But whenever you can, you go back and take a stab at the other thing. This week I made a deal to make a fascinating film. I don't think it's going to make a quarter. But if you're a producer and you like films, it's such an appealing thing to do.

When you were a boy in Boston, what made you care about movies, or what turned you on to show business?

LEVINE: I didn't get into the business until I was about to get married. I was in the restaurant business, and my wife's father didn't want her to marry anybody in the restaurant business because you wouldn't get home until two in the morning. That's how I happened to buy seven Ken Maynard Westerns, if you'll excuse the expression [the Westerns in which Maynard starred were low-budget formula pictures], and they were a disaster, but that's how I broke into the motion-picture business. And my wife's father didn't like Ken Maynard either.

You didn't particularly love movies at the time?

LEVINE: Oh, yes, but I didn't love the *business* for a long time, because it was very rugged. I didn't make any money.

You've been called a "master showman," a "promotional genius."

Do you consider the promotion of a film when you decide whether you're going to do it?

LEVINE: I believe in promotion with all my heart. We have never taken advantage of all the things that could be done in a promotional way for the movie business. Let's take *8½* [directed by Federico Fellini, Italy, 1962], which was a three-way co-production. Columbia Pictures took the whole world except for Italy. Italy was taken by producer Angelo Rizzoli. The picture did nothing in Italy. I was the co-producer for the United States and Canada. I never understood the picture, to tell you the truth, but we promoted the hell out of it. We had over a hundred screenings for different egghead types, and it became what I call a cocktail picture: "Have you seen *8½*? You *must* see it." It became the thing to do, and we did a hell of a business. Months later, Fellini was in New York and wanted to see *8½*, to look at an actor we had used, so we went to see it at a theater I owned on 57th Street. We had come to about the middle of the picture and I said, "Federico, what the hell does that mean?" He said, "I don't know."

It's said that you spent $100,000 to acquire Hercules *and $1 million to exploit it.*

LEVINE: I spent $125,000 on the picture and then I spent $1,156,000 to launch it. Now, that $1,156,000 is the same as $10 million today [in terms of the higher costs of advertising, as well as inflation]. It didn't bomb because I didn't have the $125,000 and I didn't have the $1,156,000. That isn't all of it, of course. You can only do so much with advertising. After a while, they don't believe all the lies we tell them. You have to have a film to back it up.

One day I was talking to Robert O'Brien, the president of Metro-Goldwyn-Mayer, and he told me that he had just come from Italy, where he had seen a picture called *Hercules*. It dawned on me that there had never been a picture called *Hercules*. There was a picture called *Ben-Hur*, but I didn't know who the hell Ben-Hur was and I asked a lot of kids, "Who's Ben-Hur? What does Ben-Hur do? Was he a tailor? An actor?" But every kid in the world knew who Hercules was, the strongest man in the world. Based on that alone, I went back to Italy and I saw the picture. It was terrible, so I bought it.

Listen, I love Italians, but they don't know how to dub a

picture. They couldn't care less. In Italy, if the guy says on reel number two, "I love you," it doesn't come until reel number four. Did any of you see *Hercules?* Remember when the mast fell? Well, the sound of the mast falling came about two minutes later. I was hysterical in the screening room. We had to dub Steve Reeves [who played Hercules] because his voice didn't have that godlike quality. He had a high, squeaky voice. That broke his heart. What made me buy *Hercules* was the same reason I bought Westerns: they're so powerful, they play such a vital part in our business, and they'll come back. That's why I bought it. Call it instinct.

When we launched *Hercules,* we had a luncheon at the Waldorf. I'm very good at luncheons. We had twelve hundred people there, and it was like doomsday. All the exhibitors were there, all the big shots, and they were sure that this fat little Jew was going to break his neck on that one. But the "lonely little Italian import," the critics called it, opened like an explosion. It started a whole new wave of "saturation" selling, a wonderful thing. A cigarette company wouldn't launch a cigarette and spend $5 million to advertise it and not have it available in every drug and grocery store in the country. That was the thing we used to miss in the picture business.

I caught the fancy of the business because it was at such a low ebb at that tme. My wife has been a great aid to me in the business. We believe in exploitation, and part of exploitation is to make as much excitement as possible with opening nights and parties. Most companies don't bother with that anymore. Believe me, it's important to get the name of the picture in the paper, to draw attention to it, and not let the picture walk in on rubber heels. For *Hercules,* my wife had what she called the "explodation list": the invitation to the luncheon was a simulated bomb, as big as a grapefruit, painted black. The name "Joseph E. Levine Presents" is on 494 films, so we've had plenty of excitement, and almost every film has had a party.

When you take a chance with a director who has never directed a film before, how do you protect yourself? To trust Mel Brooks, for example, on The Producers.

LEVINE: I just did it. He's not a very amusing man in person, you know, but he's been very successful. I liked the premise of what he was going to do, but what the hell? What he told me was different from what I saw on the screen.

Tony Harvey was appointed by Katharine Hepburn and Peter O'Toole to direct *The Lion in Winter*. Many times you get trapped like that. They both wanted him—why I'll never know, because he had never directed anything. He was a wonderful editor—he used to edit for David Lean. But I must tell you I was scared to death; he was a puny little guy and nervous as hell—I thought Peter would eat him for breakfast. I never thought he'd get through it, but he did. He's a wonderful director.

What do you think of Woody Allen?

LEVINE: He's a genius, a fabulous filmmaker. Years ago, I was running a company called Embassy Pictures, and the executive vice-president came into my office and said, "There's a crazy-looking guy out here with sneakers on who's been bothering me for three days. He wants to see you." I didn't even answer him. That was Woody Allen. If he hadn't worn sneakers, he'd be working for me today.

I heard that on A Bridge Too Far *you paid extremely high salaries to your stars, even though some were not on screen very long. Why?*

LEVINE: When I made *Bridge*, I hired the nine stars and then started to make a deal. There's been a lot of publicity that I paid Robert Redford $3 million and that I was going to ruin the business. Now they're paying Steve McQueen $6 million for some movie, *Tai-Pan*. [The film was not made, but McQueen still received $1 million of his fee.] When I hired Redford, even though I had everybody else in the picture, all the names I had, Redford was the key. For example, my distributor in Japan had offered me $1 million up front. But when I got Redford, he called me and offered me $2 million and I said, "It's not for sale." I sold it to him the same day for $3 million. Redford made a difference on that deal alone of $2 million, so the $3 million didn't mean a thing.

When you have a film like *A Bridge Too Far*, you depend on the foreign markets. In Japan, they like to see white people kill each other, so they'll buy any European war picture. Japan has become the second-biggest market in the world. You can gross $10 million or $12 million in Japan. I think *Star Wars* did

$50 million. I can't teach you the whole business, but if you come down tomorrow morning I'll give you another hour.

It was a miracle of direction and a miracle of planning on the part of [director] Dickie Attenborough that *A Bridge Too Far* came in on budget and on schedule. On a six-month shooting schedule, we used to feed sometimes seven thousand people in a day; we had at one time four hundred tanks that we borrowed from all the neighboring countries [the film was made in the Netherlands], and we bought a hundred and twenty-five jeeps and twenty-nine airplanes, but there was no problem afterward with selling them. To shoot with all these stars—if you were late with Jimmy Caan, you would be late for the next star who arrived. We hired Redford for five weeks. We got through with him in four weeks and six days. We had a day to spare. Everybody worked hard and it came off. If you made that picture today, there's no telling what it would cost and what kind of trouble you could get into. The only trouble we had was on a drop where we used the British paratroopers. We had bad weather three days in a row and we had to keep those guys. It cost us $1 million more than we figured, which is peanuts for that kind of a picture [the total production cost was $18 million].

Do you always stay close to a production when it's shooting?

LEVINE: I've done it various ways. Years ago before I sold the company, I used to make as many as twelve pictures at a time. I used to call myself the executive producer. I wanted to learn something about the business. On *Magic* and *Bridge,* I lived with the picture. I was on the set early in the morning with Dickie— five A.M. Nobody seemed to sleep. The only time I was out of it was when I hurt my leg and they took me home on a stretcher, but I came back in three weeks. It was a marvelous experience. What I got out of it was never to make a picture in Holland again because you even have to pay if you want to see tulips. Did you know that? There are tulip gardens, and if you want to see them you have to pay admission.

You've mostly stayed away from the studios in making your pictures.

LEVINE: No, I made *Magic* at Fox, and I thought the dining room was very good.

Do you prefer to do your own independent financing?

LEVINE: It's wonderful if you can do it. Let's take *Magic* for an example. I had a lot of takers because the script [by William Goldman, from his novel] was so good. The book was sent to everybody. When a big writer creates a book, the film rights are auctioned. The author's agents or publisher call everybody at nine A.M. and by the end of the day they've sold it. Well, everybody was bidding on *Magic*. I don't have to have a board of directors' meeting; I make a decision myself. I wanted the book very badly, so I offered $1 million, and at four forty-five P.M. I got it.

When I started the picture, several of the companies that had shown a great interest in it kept calling me to ask when I wanted to make a deal. I thought I'd wait to finish the picture. I knew it was good. All the rushes were run in the Fox screening rooms, and the operators are under their employ, so if they're worth their weight, they must tell their boss that they're looking at great rushes. Things get around in this town, and everybody knew, or thought, that we had a good picture. When you get to that point, it's very advantageous not to have committed yourself. You can make a hell of a deal.

Did you just sell them the U.S. distribution rights?

LEVINE: No, I didn't sell them anything. They distribute for you for a period of years. You try to make those years as few as possible, because everybody in the industry knows now that a picture is never dead. Negatives are always worth money, especially in these times with the advent of cable TV and regular TV, the discs and the cassettes. So you make a deal for a few years and they pay you a percentage either of the gross or the net. If you ever make a picture, forget the word "net." Never say it to yourself. Think of gross, and you'll get rich—is it all right to give that advice?

That sounds like good advice.

LEVINE: It looks like you all want to get rich.

Mr. Levine, speaking of getting rich, given the state of the industry today, can a new producer hope to accomplish half of what you have?

LEVINE: Well, why not? You're living in a marvelous country, the best country in the world—why couldn't you? I had everything stacked against me. If you want me to tell you how poor I was, you'll cry. This business, you've never had the opportunity you've got right at this minute. There are so many things going on, you can't miss. It's very difficult to lose money in this market. There are so many new technological advances. There's television, where you sell it off. Years ago if you had one winner in eight pictures, you were lucky and could get by. I think the average is less now, maybe one in ten, but today you have a shot at getting lucky and making $100 million in one shot. Look at *One Flew Over the Cuckoo's Nest*. The kid [Michael Douglas, the producer] made a fortune. If you're looking for just money.

I think the future is fantastic. Listen, for ten years I've said that the home box, pay TV, would grow to be a giant, and I lived to see it. But it's a small giant compared to what it will be five years or seven years or ten years from now. Then some of you will be producers, and you'll make a film and you'll settle for $20 million, for one night. And where are you going to get all the pictures to satisfy free TV, pay TV, and movie theaters?

The home box gives you the currency to do almost anything you want to make. You know up the line somewhere you can sell the residual rights to television. Before I started this little company I now have, I served six years of penal servitude with Avco Embassy. When I left there I was going to retire for six days, but I went to Italy and bought a film called *The Night Porter*. I did very well with it, made a lot of money, but I remember I sold the rights to the home box for $50,000. The price in those five years has escalated fifteen times. Every month they add a couple of hundred thousand homes. All the big money is going into that business. It's a tremendous business. They're going to use up pictures. You'll never be able to make enough pictures. Right now, television and pay TV haven't grown enough to play first-run pictures. I mean good films, not the crap they make for television. When pay TV gets to a point where money is no object, they're going to have millions of subscribers.

What role do you see cassettes playing?

LEVINE: Avco Embassy just made a big deal for some of its pictures. Fox quadrupled in one year, and the Japanese are sending in these machines like hotcakes. Now you've got the discs coming out. You'll be able to play a record on top of your machine that will show you a movie. The strength is with the guy who makes the film, because none of those things is any good without good film. So you'll all be rich in no time. Your mother probably wanted you to be a doctor. If I had ten kids I'd urge them all to go into this business.

Do you believe in operating out of New York?

LEVINE: Not really. I've operated all over the world. I practically lived in Italy for ten or twelve years. I made a hundred and fifty pictures in Italy.

You never thought it necessary to be in Hollywood?

LEVINE: You don't have to. There are guys in this business who don't ever come to Hollywood. *Magic* was a picture I had to make here, so I came here. If I'm going to make a pirate picture, I can't shoot it in Hollywood; I've got to shoot it either in Spain or the Bahamas. The last two pictures, *Bridge* and *Magic*, took me four years, and I can't afford that time. It was two and a half years of my life for *Bridge*, but in addition to making it, I prepared it. After it was finished, I promoted it. I did the same thing with *Magic*. That's too long. I'm not going to be as active in promotion with my next picture. That's probably a big lie.

Can an unproven writer get a script to you?

LEVINE: It's difficult now, because in fairness to the writer I have to send it back. I don't read it because even if I read it and liked it, I couldn't make it. I'm probably missing a lot of golden opportunities, but there's no way I could be doing more than I'm doing now. I don't want to have a big company. I only have ten or eleven employees now. For me, at this point, it's what I want to do. When I was younger, I wanted to conquer the world.

You've got a piece of it.

LEVINE: Yes, just a small corner in Connecticut.

Jean Renoir

No filmmaker was more loved and admired than Jean Renoir, whose extraordinarly rich body of work has been described by François Truffaut as "the most alive films in the history of the cinema, films which still breathe forty years after they were made."

Renoir, who died in 1979, made such enduring classics as *La Grande Illusion*, the 1937 antiwar film with Jean Gabin, Marcel Dalio, and Erich von Stroheim; *La Règle du Jeu (The Rules of the Game)*, the 1939 comedy-drama about a society on the brink of collapse, often considered his masterpiece; and the ravishing color films of his later period, *The River*, *The Golden Coach*, *French Cancan*, and *Picnic on the Grass*.

Renowned for his brilliance in directing actors, his adventurous and complex themes, and his mastery of technique, Renoir was revered above all else for the warm humanity of his films. As Truffaut, his friend and protégé, put it, "Renoir's work has always been guided by a philosophy of life which expresses itself with the aid of something much like a trade secret: *sympathy*."

The son of the great painter Pierre-Auguste Renoir, Jean Renoir was born in Paris in 1894 and served as a model for some of

41

his father's most celebrated paintings. His older brother, Pierre, was an actor, and a nephew, Claude, became a cameraman.

After World War I service in the French cavalry, infantry, and Air Force, Renoir dabbled in ceramics before settling on a career in films. He made his directing debut in 1924 with *La Fille de l'Eau*, starring his first wife, Catherine Hessling, with whom he made several other silent films.

Renoir's subsequent work falls into several distinct periods, including his politically engaged films of the 1930s, often shot on location; his Hollywood films of the 1940s, an uneven group reflecting his twin penchants for artifice and naturalism; and the lavishly theatrical, life-celebrating color films of the 1950s. His last film was the serenely valedictory *Le Petit Théâtre par Jean Renoir* in 1969.

But his films defy conventional classification, with their life-like blend of comedy and drama, their wide range of political and social sympathies, and their freedom in exploring diverse visual and dramatic styles. As the critic André Bazin has written, "Jean Renoir has never ceased, in the course of a long but completely uncompromising career, to search and to renew himself."

A resident of Beverly Hills, California, since 1940, when he and his second wife Dido Freire fled the Nazi invasion of France, Renoir faced increasing physical infirmity in his later years but kept his creative energies alive with a series of books fully as remarkable as his films: the memoirs *Renoir, My Father* and *My Life and My Films*, and the novels *The Notebooks of Captain Georges*, *Le Coeur à l'Aise (The Heart at Ease)*, *Le Crime de l'Anglais (The Crime of the Englishman)*, and *Geneviève*, the latter completed just a few days before his death.

FILMOGRAPHY

1924 *Catherine (Une Vie sans Joie)* (writer and actor only) / *La Fille de l'Eau*   1926 *Nana* / *Charleston*   1927 *Marquitta* / *La P'tite Lili* (actor only)   1928   *La Petite Marchande d'Allumettes* / *Tire au Flanc* / *Le Tournoi (Le Tournoi dans la Cité)*   1929 *Le Bled* / *Le Petit Chaperon Rouge* (actor only)   1930 *La Chasse à la Fortune* (actor only)   1931 *On Purge Bébé* / *La*

Chienne   1932 *La Nuit du Carrefour* / *Chotard et Cie.* / *Boudu Sauvé des Eaux*   1933 *Madame Bovary*   1934 *Toni*   1935 *Le Crime de M. Lange*   1936 *La Vie Est à Nous* (also actor) / *Une Partie de Campagne* (also actor) / *Les Bas-Fonds*   1937 *La Grande Illusion* / *La Marseillaise* / *Terre d'Espagne* (writer and narrator only)   1938 *La Bête Humaine* (also actor)   1939 *La Règle du Jeu* (also actor)   1940 *La Tosca* (with Carl Koch)   1941 *Swamp Water*   1943 *This Land Is Mine*   1944 *Salute to France*   1945 *The Southerner*   1946 *The Diary of a Chambermaid* / *The Woman on the Beach*   1950 *The River*   1952 *Le Carrosse d'Or*   1954 *French Cancan*   1956 *Eléna et les Hommes* / *L'Album de Famille de Jean Renoir* (actor only)   1959 *Le Testament du Dr. Cordelier* / *Le Dejeuner sur l'Herbe*   1962 *Le Caporal Epinglé*   1968 *La Direction d'Acteur par Jean Renoir* (actor only)   1969 *The Christian Licorice Store* (actor only) / *Le Petit Théâtre par Jean Renoir*

THE SEMINAR

Jean Renoir held a seminar with the Fellows of the Center for Advanced Film Studies on April 15, 1970.

We would like to ask you questions following a certain order having to do with the filmmaking process. Starting with the question, simply, of how do you start on an idea?

RENOIR: Well, I do start with an idea, when I can. I'm probably not the right person to answer such a question, because I spent my life suggesting stories, and nobody wanted them. It's still going on. I'm used to it and I'm not complaining, because the ideas which were forced on me were often better than my own. A mixture of what was brought to me, and what I had in my imagination, gave a happy medium which perhaps helped to make the picture a little more alive. Of course, you can always do a picture which is the expression of your personality, even if you have to work on a story you don't like very much and within a frame which seems to be very severe.

Perhaps the first thing you ask from a director is to know how to digest some types of foods which were not at all for him. You must give up, give up, give up constantly; but with the idea inside you don't give up. Apparently you do give up; but in the final result, it is your picture and *not* the picture of a neighbor. That is why I cannot give you any recipe about how to start a picture.

What is a picture? Don't be surprised if I am hesitating. I believe that a picture is a state of mind. Often a picture, when it is good, is the result of some inner belief which is so strong that you show what you want in spite of a stupid story—or in spite of a difficulty about the commercial side of the picture. Yes, it's a state of mind. The direction of the picture, the writing of the script, the cutting—all those things are one operation. It's like in literature: you start a sentence but you don't finish it because you don't find the right word. For a picture, perhaps you have to find the right word in the cutting room. A picture is a whole; you cannot say this is the beginning, this is the end, and the middle. No.

I divide directors into two categories. One category is the directors whose work starts from the camera. You put your camera in a certain spot, which is carefully chosen. It gives you a beautiful background, it gives you, with the props, a certain idea which can symbolically help the telling of the story. Then you take actors and put them in front of the lens, and you go on. That means the role of direction is based on the service of the camera. Wonderful directors work that way—René Clair, for instance. I will always remember in the silent days when I paid a visit to René Clair on the stage. He was shooting a scene with an actor—not a great actor; a good actor. In the script, the actor's jacket had to slightly brush an object on the table. I don't remember what object—maybe a statue. But the actor couldn't do it. René Clair shot the scene something like fifty times, and finally he got it; he was delighted.

But I am the opposite. I like to start with the actors. I consider that my profession as a director is not exactly like supervision. No. We are, simply, midwives. The actor has something inside himself, but very often he doesn't realize what he has in mind, in his own heart; you have to tell him. You have to help him find himself. You rehearse, and when you are happy about the rehearsal, you decide that you can give the rein to the cameraman. You ask the cameraman to come with you, the soundman to come with you, and you decide what the angle will be. But this angle depends on the acting of the actor, not on the imagination of the director. That's more my method.

Now, to talk about method in our profession is childish, because there is no method. You must change your method according to each different shot. The fact that the basis of my work is the actor made me adopt a different way of cutting the pictures, in order to help the actors. I always try not to cut the film during the shooting. That's why I so often use tracking shots, pans, and so forth. It is for no other reason than that I hate to cut the acting of an actor during his inspiration. The reason for my camerawork was to have the camera hanging on the actor, following the actor, the camera being just a recording instrument, not a god. A great director, perhaps the top director in our day, Jean-Luc Godard, is exactly the opposite of me. He starts with the camera. His frames are a direct expression of his personality without the in-between worries brought by actors—they have a headache, their wife left them, but they love her. Now, myself, since I am not Goliath but perhaps a little David, I need all those things. I need the actor who comes to me and says, "Oh, I am so unhappy—I believe my mistress is cheating me, and I cannot stand it." Well, that's my job—to open the door to such confidences and to use them for the best in my picture.

This question of the importance or nonimportance you give to the actors is exactly the quarrel which is going on in any profession in our world, between abstract art and nonabstract art. The director who is searching for an abstract emotion doesn't need forms, doesn't need the faces of actors. He can talk directly from his chest to the heart of a spectator. Myself, I am more in favor of the other method, which we could compare to figurative art in painting. That doesn't mean that you cannot interweave all sorts of methods. I want to have an idea of my scene from the rehearsal. When I have a clear idea of my scene, all of a sudden I realize everything I was doing was wrong. I start again. Finally, when the scene shows something which seems to me sufficient, I bring the camera.

In an article he did on you, director Georges Franju reported that after every take you would tell the actors—whether or not the take seemed successful—that it was in fact good but that you would rather try another interpretation. Is this a technique you have used?

RENOIR: Often, yes, yes. I hate to discourage people. The truth is, if you discourage an actor you may never find him again; you'll hide his personality behind a kind of mask, a mask of fear. We must not lose something in mind: It is that an actor is an animal, extremely fragile. You get a little expression. It's not exactly what you wanted, but it's alive. It's something human. Don't kill it. Don't kill it by pushing your own ideas into his imagination. No. Try softly, slowly, to help him to find what you believe is the truth, and which *is* the truth, because in the picture the truth is the truth of the author.

I will tell you a little story. It was during the shooting of my picture *Grand Illusion* [1937]. Perhaps some of you here know the picture. You remember at the end Jean Gabin and Marcel Dalio are walking in the snow, and Dalio is wounded. He has had a little accident and is limping. He can't go any farther. It is impossible. Well, I had written two pages of beautiful literature to explain the situation. Gabin was like a poet, explaining what's good, what's bad in nature. It was fantastic—I was so proud of myself. And I was a little worried because the two actors, Dalio and Gabin, didn't want to start the scene. They were finding reasons to do something else. Finally Gabin told me, "Jean, we'd better tell you: your two pages of beautiful poetry are just trash and we cannot say it." Which was true. I was embarrassed because it was the end of the snow season and I had to finish this sequence as fast as I could.

Finally I had an idea—oh, perhaps Dalio had the idea, perhaps Gabin. One of them was humming a tune I had already used in the beginning of the picture, "The Little Sailor." I took those innocent words, and they became the center of the scene. The scene is good, I think. But, without the reluctance of Dalio and Gabin, without my belief in the help the actors can bring you, I would have nothing. Nothing. Oh, I would have a perfectly drawn and conceived scene, but dull. There is an old slogan, very successful in our Occidental civilization, that you must look to an end higher than normal; that way you will do something, but your aim must be very, very high. Myself, I am absolutely convinced that it is mere stupidity. The aim must be easy to reach. By reaching it, you do much more. The trouble with us human beings is that we are often very stupid. Things are in front of us, and we don't see them. An actress rehearses with a beautiful face full of emotion—you don't see it, you are thinking of your camera angle. I'm not for that. I'm delighted to have the occasion sometimes to use the chance, not the planning. I'm against planning.

I'm in favor of the art and literature of the Middle Ages, up to the Renaissance. To me the Renaissance is a barbarian order which replaced a great civilization. But in the twelfth-century civilization—as it is still in India and in many parts of Asia today— you have a frame for anything. For a song, for instance, you have a frame: the legend of the *Song of Roland* was repeated and repeated and repeated by thousands, millions of people. You believe it will be monotonous. It isn't. Because inside this frame, you are free. You do what you want. I believe in this conception of art.

The Renaissance brought the cult of the individual. Well, I believe that the individual shows himself in an interesting way when he doesn't know that he shows himself. When you are in the studio and you stand beside the camera and yell, "I am going to express myself"—then you will express nothing. But if you are submerged in admiration of the beauty of the gesture of an actor—or, if it is a documentary picture, the beauty of the piece of nature that confronts you—you have a chance to show yourself behind those images more than if you want to show yourself directly. Of course, that is my opinion. I don't pretend that this opinion is right. Every one of us must build up our grammar, our method, like the recipe in a cookbook.

Do you rehearse just before you shoot, or do you begin earlier?

RENOIR: Usually when you work on a picture the money is too rare. You have to hurry. But if I had the time, I would work first in a rehearsing room with no props. That is a very old idea. The name of this kind of work is *à l'italienne*—to rehearse the Italian way. That was very much in favor in the time of *la commedia dell'arte* in Italy. They brought this method to Paris, to London. I tell you what it is: the most important characters and the director sit down around a table and you read your texts, without any expression. You must read the lines as you would read the telephone directory: *blah blah blah blah blah blah*—monotonous, flat.

Let's say we have a scene of a mother confronted suddenly with the death of her son. You ask the actress to help you find expression. The actress pulls a little drawer—a symbolic drawer—and she finds four or five expressions she's already used a hundred times, and other actors in the world have used millions of times. If you forbid her to give an expression in the beginning, the situation—the text—grows inside her. Sometimes, not often but sometimes, among the actors who are reciting this flat text, you see a little sparkle. Oh, you cannot miss it—it is the baby. The midwife did her job. When you have one proof that the sparkle does exist, you go to the stage, you rehearse, and so on. This method is never used because it takes too much time, and time is money in the picture business.

Fortunately, there were several pictures on which I could work from before the beginning. One of them that I rehearsed quite a bit was *Boudu* [*Boudu Sauvé des Eaux*, 1932], with Michel Simon. We didn't know exactly what to do with this character. He seems to be very simple. He's not simple. We worked *à l'italienne*, and one day Michel Simon got up and started to walk as Boudu and to talk with the voice of Boudu. All of a sudden: "I am Boudu. Follow me."

A picture is a little world. Something very important in life is balance. You must balance all the elements. What is very dangerous in pictures, when you work with a star, is the fact that this star became a star because of the repetition of the same voice, the same gestures. The public got used to it, and the poor soul makes millions, but doesn't make anything about talent. To me, it's something quite tragic to see a human being repeating always the same gestures, and those gestures not being even true, not being real, not being the expression of reality.

And—excuse me if I jump from one idea to another one— the camerawork is especially dangerous in this city, in Hollywood. It became so important that in the minds of many people the camerawork was the only thing which was important. On the sound stage, if you were working with an actor and everything was wrong—the actor is not satisfied, I am not satisfied—the producer would arrive and say, "Please, you are fussy, both of you; you are looking for something impossible. The shot is sufficient like that, and we must not waste time with such nonsense." But if the cameraman was looking to remove a little shadow at the tip of the nose of the star, he could take three days if he wanted.

When you shoot a tracking shot, do you also shoot other material which will allow you to shorten it later if you want, or to change the rhythm?

RENOIR: No. You should do it, but I don't. I believe it's a good thing to be committed, to play the game. You have the scene, you believe it's good: shoot it. In the studios, people want at least five takes. When I can, I have one take; I like to be the slave of my decision. If I know I won't have those shots to cut, my main shot will be better. If I know I will have those shots, I say, "Oh, that's not very good—but we'll have the close shots." I don't like this attitude.

Often I don't understand the problems of a shot before it is shot. When we are ready to shoot—the lights are burning, the cameras are ready, everything is ready—all of a sudden you think of something which was obvious, and you didn't see it. You realize that the girl should have no hat, and instead of acting the scene standing and nervous, she should sit down and stay still. You have to change, too. It's why I cannot decide in advance if the scene will be with many shots, or with only one main shot. To be frank, I don't like too many close shots. When I started in this business, my first preoccupation was to find lenses which could allow me to have the background clear, not out of focus. I hate to show people who seem to be just out of an icebox, sterilized. I like a little dirt from the outside to give some life to my shots. I believe the ideal work is to prepare the shot, to be ready to shoot it, to be perfectly satisfied, and then to understand the element you are missing, and to add this element.

It is exactly like with old buildings. You buy an old farm in the Midwest that you want to fix for living in. Probably you will get something much more alive than if you start from your own plans with a new house. Very often I wonder if it's not the same thing with women. No, I'm not joking. With the woman you love, with the house you love, with a piece of furniture you love, there is something which is not exactly dust, it's not exactly worn out, it's not exactly the fact that the lock is broken. No. There is some life which comes mysteriously. It's like a coating, and the objects missing this coating are dull. There is nothing sadder than a new apartment without it.

How do you work with the art directors of your pictures? How much control do you exercise over the sets and the colors, and what guides you in your decisions?

RENOIR: I like to have control on every part of the picture: the art directors, the cameramen, the actors. I like to know intimately what they do, and to suggest, to help them to decide when there is a choice. But I don't believe in specialists. It can happen that an actor will tell me, "I don't like this part of the set." We have a discussion about it, and change it if necessary. In other words, I like to keep the right of the important decisions and also the details, but I don't like to do it alone. I like to feel that around my direction many other problems are going on, and that I know them and am participating, as the technicians or the actors are participating in my worries. I believe in this world we proceed by little groups. You must belong to a little group. That doesn't mean that you lose your individuality, not at all. Belonging to a little group helps you find it.

In creating a scene—in writing and directing it—what do you look for?

RENOIR: I will try to answer your question, which is a very difficult question. You must excuse me if I go back to *Grand Illusion*. This film was not based on the pleasure of reviving a period which was a very tough period, but of reviving a period in which I met quite interesting people. The people who were in the Air Force, for instance, were perfectly interesting, quite amusing. Also, I shot *Grand Illusion* because I was mad at a certain patriotic caricature which became very successful after the Armistice, showing the people a kind of cliché about soldiers at war. I can give you a typical example of this cliché. The newspaper people, and the people who wrote screenplays during the First World War and right after, used an expression when they were talking about the Germans which was very disparaging: *les Boches*. Many people didn't say *les Allemands*. They used to say *les Boches*, being sure to use a kind of slang of the front, thinking that the soldiers in the trenches were also talking about *Boches*, which was not true. I was in the war, and I heard it the first time, I believe, at Maxim's, in Paris. The word we used for the Germans was *Fridolins* [derived from the German name "Fritz"]: "The *Fridolins* are a little nervous tonight." In the picture I wanted to show people at war as I knew them, not as some patriotic writers used to make them. Also, in *Grand Illusion* Gabin is wearing the jacket I had in the Air Force during the war.

I will tell you how I made this picture. I was shooting *Toni* [1934] in the south of France. I made *Toni* almost entirely on location. Nearby was a big military airfield. The pilots could see that somebody was shooting a picture: the reflectors, the cameras, the trucks. They were above my head the whole day long. I couldn't record any sound. I decided to pay a visit to the commanding officer of this base, and I was confronted by a man who was a very good friend of mine. As a matter of fact, during the First World War he saved my life several times. He was a fighter in a squadron of fighting planes. I was a photographer. That's the way I became interested in movies, by taking photographs from above. Planes carrying cameras were not very fast; each time we were confronted by a German fighter we thought that was the end. Several times my general—who was just a non-com at the time—arrived with his little squad and *tak-tak-tak*, the Germans were happy to run away. This is why I consider that this man saved my life several times. His name was Pinsard. He's dead now.

General Pinsard had been shot down by the Germans seven times. He escaped seven times, and went back to his squadron seven times. We were happy to find each other, to meet again. We were the habit of having dinner together in a little joint. During these dinners he told me the story of how he escaped from the German jails. I thought that could be a good suspense story, an escape story. I asked his permission to use a few of the stories he had told me. I wrote a screenplay, convinced I had written a very banal escape story. I thought it was very commercial, very popular, and that I could find the financing very easily. That's what I thought. During three years, my dear friends, I visited every office on the Champs Elysées or in Rome, or anywhere. Everywhere I had the same answer: "No girls in your picture and we are not interested." Good. Finally an answer to your first question: you wanted to know how I start a production.

I met a man who was—well, I don't like to insult people, but I don't find any other word but the word "crook." He was a brilliant, successful crook; that was his profession. He told me he just had made several millions with an operation. I don't know which one—I don't understand anything about such things. He told me, "Jean, I believe in your picture." I said, "That is because you are not in the film business—people in the film business don't believe in it." "That doesn't matter. How much do you want?" I needed 2 million old francs, real francs. He said, "OK, you will have them. Let's have an agreement." I shot the picture and the picture was successful.

You were going to talk about how you work on a scene.

RENOIR: Yes. Now, the screenplay I wrote, of course, didn't follow the adventure of Pinsard. That's what I wanted to tell you: I discovered that *Grand Illusion* had another meaning. I discovered that *Grand Illusion* was perhaps a little approach to a big problem, which is the problem of nations, and which is the racist problem, the problem of how people from different religions meet, how they can understand each other, how they cannot understand each other for some other reasons. *Grand Illusion* became this question—I am crazy about such questions—to me, the only thing which is important in the world is how to meet. *Grand Illusion* was a possibility to tell everything I had in my heart about this question. But when I wrote the screenplay, I didn't know. It was just an escape story. In certain scenes between Pierre Fresnay and Erich von Stroheim, we talk only of questions of surrounding, questions of adaptation, questions of how to get along together; but I don't ever forget that it was an escape story. And the escape story was insignificant. You understand what I mean by that? It is that, by working on the picture, what I was writing was pulling out of myself ideas that were more important than I thought in the beginning.

When you had an additional idea—on racism, on how people meet, and so forth—did you then try to make a scene out of it? Could you give an example?

RENOIR: For instance, I have a scene between Dalio and Gabin when they are preparing a rope to escape. They talk, frankly, about racists. It seems that this doesn't belong to the picture, but it does. It works. I had entire scenes which were done only to express this question of origin, nation, races. I have a scene of half a dozen French prisoners preparing a show; they are sewing costumes and so forth. They have a very serious conversation having nothing to do with the scenery, with the costumes, with the show. It is a question of where are you going, where do you come from. I could put fifty situations like that into the shell of my picture. You have to break the shell to find what you are filling it with.

In introducing ideas such as these into a structure, is it not difficult sometimes sometimes to do so without stopping the picture totally, or losing interest?

RENOIR: It is terribly difficult. The problem is the change of style. But in *Grand Illusion* the setup [a military prison] is an ideal one for some discussions. *Grand Illusion* was a very easy picture to shoot and to write. The situations are obvious. *The Rules of the Game* [*La Règle du Jeu*, 1939], in which I had practically the same problem, was more difficult. I wrote a first draft in which the individual was a little gray, out of focus. I had given too much importance, again, to the outside: the life of a rich man, his mistress, the chateau where he's living. I was hoping I could do something light, elegant, and amusing with such a background. It was while I was shooting that I discovered, for instance, that the part of Christine [Nora Grégor as the wife of the wealthy man, Marcel Dalio] is a heartbreaking part.

So you set out to make a light story and it became something more?

RENOIR: Yes, but that happens to me all the time. For instance, *La Chienne* [1931]. The head of the studio [Roger Richebé], a very nice boy who wouldn't kill an elephant, gave me the money to shoot this picture with the idea that it was going to be a hilarious farce. Of course I didn't contradict him, being sure that if he knew the truth I would have to stop shooting. He realized that I was shooting a somber drama when everything was shot. He told me, "At least I want to try to save the situation, and you won't do the cutting." I said, "OK, I won't do the cutting." We started a fight with our fists. I was stronger than he was. But the next day when I went to the studio, I found a policeman who very politely said, "Monsieur Renoir, no, no, no. It is forbidden." I was saved by a wonderful man, the man who was making the money for the studio—Monsieur Monteux, the president of the most important shoe company in France. This man who understood so very much about shoes, it seemed to me he also understood about pictures. He was indignant. I was restored to my cutting room with only a few shots missing.

I made about forty films in my career, and finally the examination of my whole work is highly in favor of the way I did produce; but I owe the possibility of doing my films with so much liberty to the most unexpected producers in the world.

What is the origin of the character Octave—the one you play yourself—in Rules of the Game?

RENOIR: I thought certain situations needed a comment, and that I should add to my story a kind of master of ceremonies, like in a revue on the stage. I found out that this master of ceremonies would have to say everything that I myself, the author, had in mind. I said, "Well, why not say it myself?"

He is a special character in that he passes from one class to another.

RENOIR: Yes, because he practically is a tramp—the tramp in the tuxedo.

Did you have him in mind when you began to write the picture?

RENOIR: No. I found him before finishing the script—I had about half of the script.

How do you go about casting?

RENOIR: I like to have my friends—technicians and other people—help me, because I am very bad at casting. Sometimes to be bad helps me, in the way that I am attracted by a certain innocence. I am afraid of clichés, tricks; I am afraid of repeating situations we have already seen on the screen. People who do not have too much skill sometimes help me keep a kind of—I use a very ambitious word, excuse me—a kind of innocence.

When you have a difficult actor—people say Stroheim was difficult—how do you try to come to an agreement with him?

RENOIR: It's a kind of a compromising. I never found an actor in complete opposition to me. Never. If that's been the situation, I don't know it. I work with people who have the reputation of being impossible. I've found them delightful. I believe that everything must come from inside the individual. Again, I use the comparison of the midwife. If you tell an actor, "You must do that—that—here, you will scratch your nose," he will be bad. An actor must find for himself all those things. An actor must have the feeling that he wrote the part. It's not true; he didn't write it—but he must believe it. He must reject what doesn't seem to come from him. Of course that brings discussions, but out of those discussions sometimes you find a big improvement in the scene.

Too many directors work the following way: they tell the actor, "Sit down, my dear friends, and look at me. I am going to act a scene, and you are going to repeat what I did." He acts a scene and he acts badly, because if he is a director instead of an actor it's probably because he's a bad actor.

I don't want an actor to imitate me. There is no reason why all of a sudden an actor should be Jean Renoir on the screen. There is no reason why there should be another one. After all, the purpose of art, and also the purpose of moviemaking, is to find yourself. If you are looking for a character who doesn't exist in life, an ideal character you build in your imagination, that's wrong. If you can prove to the actor that it's false, the actor will be the first to look for something else—and perhaps to find it.

When you have an actor who is overplaying, how do you deal with him?

RENOIR: Number one, I don't believe that an actor can over-act. To me, if an actor is on the right track—that is, his creation is a real human being—he cannot do too much. If he is on the wrong track, even if he hardly moves the lips he is bad.

When you are confronted with an actor who has not found the right track, what might you say?

RENOIR: If you are involved in the picture, you cannot go back. What is shot is shot. You can never replace it. What you have to do is try to find a way to match your ideas with the exaggerations of this actor. It's more difficult with parts that have little dialogue. But if you have enough dialogue to allow an actor to play with the words to his discretion, unless he is a perfect idiot—or unless *you* are a perfect idiot, which may also happen—you always find a way, a happy medium.

A number of your pictures deal with the theater, with the lives of actors, such as The Golden Coach [Le Carrosse d'Or, *1952*]. *Could you talk about the way theater relates to the way you view film?*

RENOIR: Well, you know, I cannot answer your question directly, because I shot *The Golden Coach* almost twenty years ago. I have forgotten my state of mind during this period, but I can relate your question to a big question which I am asking myself constantly. Perhaps it is the most important preoccupation regarding filmmaking I've had in my life. It is the quesion of the outside reality and the inside reality. Let me give you an example: you have an actor who must play the part of a sailor. Being very conscientious, he will buy the real costume of a sailor. He will wear a cap which went through the tempests and hurricanes of the sea. He will, perhaps, live on a boat to get used not only to the language of sailors but to have the bronzed skin of a man who constantly lives outside. He will act the part, and he will look exactly like a ham, because he is not a good actor. That's one thing. Now, if you suggest to another actor—Charlie Chaplin—that he should play the part of a sailor, even with a cane and derby he will be a sailor.

In your earlier pictures, particularly the ones that historians have chosen to call "realist," there often is a tone of anger, an undercurrent of protest. Starting with The Golden Coach, *especially, your films have a great joy in them, a kind of celebration of life. I wonder if you might comment on this transition.*

RENOIR: It is true, I shot many pictures out of anger. But probably there is as much anger in *The Golden Coach.*

I don't think I saw the anger in it.

RENOIR: Well, *The Golden Coach* is a picture about a certain society, and to me this picture is no more encouraging than any somber drama. I don't know how to make differences between drama, comedies, tragedies; to me it's all the same.

Do you feel that in your own work you attempt to get audience sympathy or involvement with a main character? Do you feel this is necessary in order for your films to work?

RENOIR: No, nothing is necessary. What you say can help. Why not accept any help? Of course we all want it. You are in a preview. Your picture is a little dull. The public doesn't follow very well. All of a sudden on the screen some actor cracks a joke which you wrote unwillingly, but you had to do something, you had to fill a space. You hear a little laughter among the audience. You feel like a million. You are delighted. You would like to see who laughed—to kiss him. Yes, we depend on the public. What is wrong is to believe that the public must be a crowd of millions of people. For some artists, the public is ten people, or one person. The size of the crowd isn't important. What is important is that you are in communication with somebody, with a spirit which is not your spirit, but which can influence you for a short time. Now, I repeat—and excuse me if I repeat myself so often—those are my ideas, but that doesn't mean they are good. Tomorrow I will perhaps have different ideas. I am not steady. You know, I don't believe that a man is more steady than a tree. We change. And our ideas change.

But, of course, you have to think of the public. I have a nephew [Claude Renoir] who is a cameraman. A few years ago he made an extraordinary picture about Picasso [*Le Mystère Picasso*, 1956, directed by Henri-Georges Clouzot]. He had a transparency, and Picasso was on the other side of the screen, painting. You see the beginning of a painting, a painting of not too great importance, of course, but you see the progression. During his exercise, he was repeating something which to me is a big secret we should all share and use if we can: "Fill it." Those were his words. No empty space. You have a frame. The frame is a scene in a movie or the frame of a painting. You must fill this frame. You must give the feeling that the frame is too narrow. I agree with Picasso very much.

You know what is my preoccupation in pictures, when the picture is finished? It is that I would like the picture to give the feeling to the audience that it is unfinished. Because I believe that the work of art where the spectator does not collaborate is not a work of art. I like the people who look at the picture, perhaps, to build a different story on the side. That was the marvelous thing in the silent days: you had to build your own dialogue. You were collaborating. You can't do it today. But without any collaboration of the public, to me, we have nothing. What is good is when the public says, "Oh, that couple didn't get along. The wife was disgusting." A man says, "No, no. The wife is not disgusting. I like her. She must have reasons. I'm sure she was very unhappy when she was a little girl." You start to build stories around the story. That's a good picture. We must be in communion, the artist and the public. We must arrive at the point where the public is the maker, and the artist becomes the spectator. But, you notice, I'm just dreaming aloud now.

THE SCREENWRITER
Robert Towne

Producer Robert Evans, for whom Robert Towne wrote the Oscar-winning original screenplay of *Chinatown*, once said, "I would rather have the next five commitments from Robert Towne than the next five commitments from Robert Redford."

Generally considered the finest contemporary Hollywood screenwriter, Towne made his reputation within the industry as an uncredited "script doctor" on *Bonnie and Clyde* and *The Godfather*, but it was the 1974 detective film *Chinatown* that brought him wider fame. Since then Towne has written *Shampoo* with actor-producer Warren Beatty, and in 1982 he made his debut as a writer-director on *Personal Best*.

Born in Los Angeles in the mid-1930s, Towne was raised in the fishing port of San Pedro, where he worked as a tuna fisherman. After army service, Towne joined Jeff Corey's Hollywood acting workshop in 1958, where he met Jack Nicholson (later to star in his screenplays of *The Last Detail* and *Chinatown*) and producer-director Roger Corman. Corman gave Towne his start as a screenwriter on the horror movies *The Last Woman on Earth* (1960) and *Tomb of Ligeia* (1964).

After an unhappy experience writing episodic television,

61

Towne was brought by Beatty to the Texas location of *Bonnie and Clyde* for a final rewrite on the David Newman-Robert Benton screenplay. He performed another valuable last-minute job on *The Godfather,* writing the crucial final scene between Marlon Brando and Al Pacino on the night before the shooting.

Director-screenwriter Francis Coppola, accepting his Oscar for best screenplay of *The Godfather,* thanked Towne for his contribution. But Towne, a meticulous craftsman, felt he was in danger of remaining a "sub-rosa creature" with his ghostwriting and his decision to remove his name from such disappointing films as *Cisco Pike* and *The New Centurions.*

His major break came in 1973 when he adapted Darryl Ponicsan's novel *The Last Detail* for Nicholson and director Hal Ashby. Towne was Evans's first choice to do the 1974 screen adaptation of *The Great Gatsby,* but he turned down the offer in order to write *Chinatown.* Towne's biggest commercial success came with *Shampoo* (1975). The comedy-drama about a philandering Beverly Hills hairdresser was in the works for so many years that the original title of the Towne-Beatty screenplay was *Hair.*

Personal Best, Towne's film about two female track stars, was a critical success, but to preserve his control over the editing he was forced to relinquish another cherished project, *Greystoke,* his version of the Tarzan story. It was filmed in 1982–83 by director Hugh Hudson, with Towne taking his credit under a pseudonym.

FILMOGRAPHY

1960 *The Last Woman on Earth* 1964 *The Tomb of Ligeia*
1967 *Bonnie and Clyde* (uncredited) 1968 *Villa Rides!* 1970
Drive, He Said (actor only) 1971 *Cisco Pike* (uncredited) 1972
The Godfather (uncredited) / *The New Centurions* (uncredited)
1973 *The Last Detail* 1974 *Chinatown* 1975 *The Yakuza* /
Shampoo 1982 *Personal Best* (also director) 1983 *Greystoke*
(under pseudonym)

THE SEMINAR

Robert Towne held seminars with the Fellows of the Center for Advanced Film Studies on January 22, 1975, and October 13, 1976.

Let's begin with the already famous ending of Chinatown *[directed by Roman Polanski, 1974]. The ending on the screen, in which Faye Dunaway is shot, isn't the one you originally wrote— Polanski intervened.*

TOWNE: As I originally wrote it, *Chinatown* didn't end in Chinatown. In fact, there wasn't one scene that took place there. But one horrible day at the studio about two weeks before shooting, everybody went crazy, and someone said, "My God, there's no scene in Chinatown, and it's called *Chinatown*." Of course I felt that was fine, and in a way the point: it was not a location but a state of mind. To have a scene there would be pushing the metaphor. "Chinatown" is meant to suggest a place where a guy thought he knew the rules of the game but discovered that he didn't, and to suggest that appearances and reality are not the same. At a deeper level, it's meant to suggest futility of good intentions: no matter what he did, it was wrong.

The meeting was insane. Somebody even said, "Well, maybe if Gittes [Jack Nicholson] liked Chinese food . . ." Finally, at this meeting, where some normally very bright people lost their heads, it was collectively agreed—but not by me—that the film should end in Chinatown.

In your original version, who killed whom?

TOWNE: Originally, I had Evelyn [Faye Dunaway] kill her father [John Huston]. Gittes tried to stop her but was too late. But he did succeed in getting her daughter out of the country. So the ending was bittersweet in that one person at least—the child— wasn't tainted. The one thing the woman had been trying to do— the purest motive in the whole film—was to protect her daughter. When she carried out this motive by killing her father, she was acting out of motherly love. You knew she was going to stand trial, that she wouldn't tell why she did it, and that she would be punished. But the larger crime—the crime against the whole community—would go unpunished. And, in a sense, that was the point.

There are some crimes for which you get punished, and there are some crimes that our society isn't equipped to punish, and so we reward the criminals. In this case, greedy men displaced a whole community and took the land. So there's really nothing to do but put their names on plaques and make them pillars of the community. It was this balance I was looking for.

Did you rewrite the ending yourself?

TOWNE: More or less, though I was arguing while I was doing it. I don't mean this unkindly, but I think it was impossible for Roman to come back to Los Angeles and not end his movie with an attractive blonde lady being murdered.

A very tricky thing happens when you're doing a film. A director comes along, and you recognize that a transference has to take place, and he has to conceive of the film as his film. You just hope that your vision will complement his and that they will be consistent with each other. So I said OK, and the film ends the way it does. My own feeling is if a scene is relentlessly bleak—as the revised ending is—it isn't as powerful as it can be if there's a little light there to underscore the bleakness. If you show something decent happening, it makes what's bad almost worse.

For example, *The Last Detail* [a Towne screenplay, adapted from the novel by Darryl Ponicsan; directed by Hal Ashby, 1973] ends up badly, but along the way there is a certain amount of warmth, friendship, good times, a concern for each other, people being decent. This serves to accentuate that in the end all those things go by the boards. If there's going to be a tunnel at the end of the light, you want to have some light before you get there. In a melodrama, where there are confrontations between good and evil, if the evil is too triumphant it destroys your ability to identify with it rather than if its victory is only qualified. I'm making no relationship to anything I've done, but if you read a great tragedy like *King Lear*, you see that what makes it so effective are all the little kindnesses along the way, the Fool and Cordelia, the virtuous daughter. Ultimately, goodness gets destroyed, but its ongoing presence lends a reality to the presence of evil.

How did you take the changes in Chinatown?

TOWNE: It was heartbreaking. But there's no way out of it with films because they are collaborative. You can't pretend they're not. You can just hope that what your quarrels are about is not the central vision but the ways of getting there.

I hadn't seen the movie for a long time until recently, and I thought it was a better movie than I had thought when I first saw it. Roman did a terrific job. But when it came out, I was filled with disappointment. I had disagreements with Roman throughout in terms of the nature of relationships between people. Let me give you one example. I must preface it by saying that I think Faye Dunaway did an extraordinary job in the picture and handled the most difficult scene, the revelation of her incest with her father, in a way that made it utterly credible.

However, I always saw that character as a sort of California Yankee, peaches and cream, infuriatingly healthy, no makeup, nothing is wrong with her. A lower-class guy who is made to feel like a pimp and a creep in her presence is driven mad with the thought that there's something wrong with her; he is having a hard time finding it, he is becoming more and more fascinated with her, and he falls in love with her. Then he finds out she's been fucking her father.

I wanted that to come out of left field. I wanted the young woman in that part not to look as ostensibly neurotic as Roman wanted Faye to look, not lacquered and marceled. So we argued about her makeup. "Everybody wore their makeup that way," Roman would say. "No, they didn't, Roman." "Well, *I* think so." You can't imagine the number of things you can disagree with on a movie, and yet, if there is a central vision, which he had, still have it turn out well.

How did Chinatown *come about? Was it your idea?*

TOWNE: Yes. It came about because Columbia decided to put off the filming of *The Last Detail*. At that point there was a counterreformation going on in which it was felt that movies were getting much too permissive and had to clean up their act. The studio was suddenly frightened of anything in which the language was socially taboo or the scenes were sexually explicit. But I wouldn't change the language in the script, and I had some leverage then at Columbia because Jack Nicholson was willing to go along with what I wanted. So it was sort of a Mexican standoff. Meanwhile, I conceived of a detective film because I wanted to direct. I thought that no matter how bad a director I was, at least if I could tell a detective story, I could keep people interested. But once you say you want to do a detective movie, you start thinking about crime, what it means to you, what you think really is a crime, what angers you. The destruction of the land and the destruction of a community was something I thought was hideous. It was doubly significant because it was the way Los Angeles was formed.

Is it the concept or the characters you begin with when you're thinking about a screenplay?

TOWNE: I don't know. You just start fishing around. In the case of *Chinatown,* two things really triggered it. In 1969 there was an article in *West* magazine, which is now defunct, called "Raymond Chandler's L.A." There were photographs of Los Angeles, taken today but showing locations as they existed then. I said, "Jesus, you could really shoot the city as it existed thirty-five years ago." The other was my memory of how certain other sections used to look, and I was very sad about many of the changes—and angry in some cases.

What sources did you use?

TOWNE: I started with Carey McWilliams's book *Southern California: An Island on the Land* [1946], then went to Morrow Mayo's *Los Angeles* [1933] and several tracts. I read some of the Department of Water and Power's own accounts which rationalized and justified what happened. At one point, if I hadn't called the picture *Chinatown,* I would have called it *Water and Power.* I talked to a couple of people in the Water Department, one of whom got very angry, and who'd been there at the time. I must have read accounts in at least a dozen different places, including Mary Austin's fictionalized version in *The Ford* [1917].

Did you draw on the research for particular scenes or locations?

TOWNE: No. A lot of the riverbed material, for example, came about because I lost a dog and was chasing it down a riverbed near Downey. I grew up in San Pedro, and a lot of the locations that I wrote in I chose because I knew they were there and I knew that they hadn't changed.

Did you have any collaboration with Richard and Anthea Sylbert, who did such fine work on the period setting and costuming?

TOWNE: Not specifically. They just made everything better.

For example, they insisted—on principle—on playing down the period, on not being obtrusive or pushy in dressing people in the style. If you look at a movie made in 1937, nobody does a close-up of the dashboard and says, "Oh, we've got a 1937 car." It was very much in the Sylberts' minds to work that way. Anthea is terrific in her sense of the makeup people should use. She also had battles with Roman over Faye Dunaway's makeup. The Sylberts are extraordinary. They always make contributions beyond their own work. On *Shampoo* [written by Towne with actor-producer Warren Beatty; directed by Hal Ashby, 1975] I would find myself, as I was rewriting, showing scenes to Anthea before anybody else, to get not just what she thought about costumes but about the characters too. On a movie set, somebody's the director and somebody's the set designer. But people do have ideas about other things, and sometimes they're very valuable.

Let's return to the origins of Chinatown. *Whom did you first approach with the idea?*

TOWNE: I was working on the screenplay, and I was slowly going broke. Paramount had asked me to adapt *The Great Gatsby*, and I told Robert Evans, who was then head of the studio, that I didn't want to do it, and he was mystified. He said, "Well, what are you doing that's so important you don't want to adapt *The Great Gatsby*?" I said, "I'm doing this detective movie." He liked it and was very interested in doing it, but I didn't take him up on it right away. About a month later, I was desperate and said, "If you still like it, we'll go ahead with it." [Evans was the producer of *Chinatown*.] He was enthusiastic, very supportive, and yet he left me alone. But I knew any hope I had of directing it was over.

What was the genesis of J. J. Gittes?

TOWNE: In most detective movies I have ever seen—in Chandler and even Dashiell Hammett—all the detectives are too gentlemanly to do divorce work: "If you want someone for that, go down the block." But I knew in fact that's mostly what they did. That's how they made their money, and it's a wonderfully seamy thing to do. So I went down the block for Gittes. I thought that taking someone like that, maybe venal and crude and used to petty crime and people cheating on each other, and then getting him involved in a crime which was really evil and allowing him to see the larger implications and then to draw the distinctions would be interesting.

He's a detective who's not always very capable. Sometimes he's pretty sloppy.

TOWNE: Yes. But very persistent and insatiably curious. And capable within certain limits.

A nosy detective? Was the slitting of his nostril and the bandaged nose your idea or Polanski's?

TOWNE: Mine, though it does seem like something Roman would have thought of. I felt it would be hard to take seriously any violence that was visited on the hero when you know he's going to last until the end of the movie. The only thing you can really be afraid for is his psychic safety, either emotional or moral. You might be afraid that he'll fall in love with the wrong person or that he'll do something so wrong you'll no longer be able to identify with him. But I wanted some violence in it because it goes with the genre, though I didn't want the conventional beating because that you don't care about. In the script I had the detective with the bandage on and the stitches on, but the smart thing Roman did was to follow right through with it, to not back off from it, to make it prominent. I think this was very shrewd of him.

Chinatown *is, for many people, a demanding film with a complicated plot. Do you agree?*

TOWNE: Maybe the story *is* too complex, I don't know. It's the kind of movie, for example, that should never be seen in a drive-in. You've got to watch everything. I think the movie's right on the edge in terms of its plot complexity. Some people say they can follow it, other people say they had difficulty with it. But I do think it's as lucid an exposition of that kind of convoluted story as you're going to get. Whether the story is too complicated to be told is another question.

A couple of scenes were cut that might have made the film a little clearer. Why were they dropped?

TOWNE: A couple of scenes which were cut did have information that would've made the movie clearer. But you have to deal with the rhythms of the movie; and the rhythms of the movie, everybody felt, worked better without the scenes.

And there was a scene I understand underwent considerable

change—the scene with Jack Nicholson and Faye Dunaway in bed together.

TOWNE: My least favorite in the film. As written initially, it was just the opposite of what was filmed. Originally, Evelyn was very disturbed by the sex and didn't lie back and say, "Gee, tell me about yourself." She was extremely upset and was actually out of bed, smoking. And Gittes was upset because he had just made love with her, and she was rejecting him. I think the original line was "Mrs. Mulwray, I hope it was something I said." Frankly, I would have preferred that—she was disturbed by the sex, and she still embodied a mystery—rather than to have her compliment Gittes for making love to her. I thought it was important to continue the mystery of the woman as he was getting more and more fascinated with her and was falling in love.

Why was it changed?

TOWNE: Roman just didn't like it that way. I think, perhaps, he preferred identifying with the character when the woman praised him for making love well. I don't know—I'm only conjecturing.

In the same scene, are his lines about having once tried to save a woman in Chinatown your lines?

TOWNE: Roman and I had a big argument about it. I don't know whether Roman was right or not. Initially, I was more specific about the story in Chinatown. I wanted what had happened to Gittes to be ridiculous—a humiliation—and instead Roman wanted to emphasize the tragedy, but he didn't want to be specific about it. I wanted Gittes to go to pains to avoid another humiliation and then have it repeat itself, not foolishly, but tragically, sadly. Roman wanted the tragedy repeated—a tragedy and then a tragedy.

When you had these standoffs with Polanski, did he always win? Did Robert Evans mediate?

TOWNE: There were certain battles where I had a limited amount of success, but basically Roman would get his way. Bob Evans's position—he is right in this—is that you take Roman as he is, or you fire him. Roman's strength is that he is what he is, and it's also his weakness, because someone like this can be terribly rigid and subject to ossification.

Besides writing original screenplays, you've also had a successful

*career as a script doctor. When you were brought in to doctor
the script of* The Godfather *[the screenplay by Francis Coppola
and Mario Puzo, from Puzo's novel, was directed by Coppola,
1972; Towne was uncredited], were you given certain sections or
the entire screenplay?*

TOWNE: I was given certain sections. The main problem was
that there was no final scene between Michael Corleone [Al Pa-
cino] and his father [Marlon Brando]. Since he was about four
or five weeks into shooting, Francis Coppola didn't know what
to do about it. He was under tremendous pressure and he could
no longer write under those conditions. He kept saying, "I want
a scene where they say they love each other." I couldn't write a
scene with two people saying they love each other. It had to be
about something, an action. So that scene in the garden between
Al Pacino and Marlon Brando is what I ended up doing—a scene
about the transfer of power. There were other little things I did,
but they were inconsequential.

What was your responsibility on Bonnie and Clyde *[directed by
Arthur Penn, 1967]?*

TOWNE: That was a lot more complicated. It was a long process. I was on the film for about three weeks of pre-production
and all the way through the shooting.

*But David Newman and Robert Benton received the only writ-
ing credits.*

TOWNE: That was a peculiar situation. And I don't know what
would have happened if it had been arbitrated, which Warren
Beatty [who produced and starred in the film] asked me not to
do. The Writers Guild rules specify that 33 percent of a script
has to be changed before credit can be given, and I really can't
say what the final result would have been. But none of it would
ever have been examined so closely if the film had not enjoyed
the success it did.

Were your changes mostly structural or in dialogue?

TOWNE: Both. I thought it was a terrific script when I first
read it, but it was unformed. It all centered on a *ménage à trois*
among Bonnie [Faye Dunaway], Clyde [Beatty], and C.W. [Mi-
chael J. Pollard], in which Clyde was not merely impotent, but a
homosexual involved with C.W. But at the time I think there were
two considerations. One was that I doubt if Warners would have

made it that way. The other was that it got static. It got to be like a series of vaudeville routines—now they're in bed with so-and-so, now they're in bed with so-and-so. Although those scenes were very amusing they didn't go anywhere ultimately. What was valuable was to try to resolve the relationship between *two* people in the course of the film. And because the film had a lot of banks to rob along the way, dealing with two people was a formidable task all by itself. So both Warren and Arthur Penn judged the script to be in trouble. This was when I was asked to come in.

You saw the couple's relationship as the key element?

TOWNE: You always knew they were going to die, so the real suspense was how, and if they were going to get something resolved between them before they died. In order to do that, you had to structure their relationship toward their particular fate. Remember the scene with Eugene the undertaker and Velma [Gene Wilder and Evans Evans]? It's a terrific scene which was unchanged from the original script. After this scene, after they've been clowning around and having hamburgers and getting very cozy with each other, somebody asks Eugene what he does. He says he's an undertaker, and Bonnie says, "Get him out of here." The scene originally took place after she'd seen her mother. The first structural change I made was to put that scene before she'd seen her mother, so that the raucous escapade with the mortician brings home the fact she's afraid she's going to die and wants to see her mother. Then rather than have the family reunion happy, as it originally was, after Clyde said, "Well, we don't want to live more than three miles away," I had the mother reply, "If you try and live three miles from me, you won't live long." All these avenues which Bonnie might have thought were still open were slowly being closed. The two were thrown more and more back on themselves and on the peculiar kind of intimacy they had between them.

You added new scenes?

TOWNE: The scene in which he made love with her was a new scene. The scene in the hotel room in which she says, "I thought we were going someplace but this is just it, and we're going," was a new scene. I can't remember all of them. I was in a hotel room working on scenes every day, and I would be told, "Try it this way." My overall impression was feeling like a fool—it was one of my first jobs—because I was asked to rewrite scenes so many times, the original and my own too. I thought, "Jeez, I must be terrible," because Arthur Penn kept asking me to do it again and again. Then I realized Arthur was really using me the way a good director uses an actor: "Try the scene this way. Try the scene that way." It was very intelligent of him.

What do you find are the most common problems in working as a script doctor?

TOWNE: "Doctoring" is misleading because all scripts are rewritten, including your own. A script *has* to be rewritten. It's just a question of whether or not it's going to be rewritten well.

One of the frustrating things about working on movies, and one of the exciting things, is that you never have the same problems twice—which is not to say there aren't certain principles. Generally speaking, scripts are too talky. And when there's a problem, it's usually because the script lacks clarity. Sometimes when creative people are insecure, they can get esoteric and be afraid to be understood. One of the great things about Roman Polanski is that he strives to be understood. I think that is the mark of anybody who's really gifted.

But the problem in a scene isn't always clear.

TOWNE: One thing I've discovered is that if a scene doesn't work one way, do the exact opposite of what you've been doing, no matter how insane it seems, and it'll sometimes work. Maybe there's a scene where a man is on his knees to a woman, begging her to come back to him. It doesn't work, so instead you have him beat her up and tear up the house. It's another way of asking her to come back. Sometimes doing just the opposite works for reasons which I can't altogether understand. Each of us has a vision of life, and part of the process of writing is not so much to explain your vision but to discover it.

Whether it's my own material or somebody else's, I ask myself what the scene is really about—not the events, but the subtext—and try to do it as simply as possible. As far as how you initially go about reworking someone else's material, I read the script like somebody trying to watch the movie. My responses are on an emotional level: I'm disturbed because a character didn't do something I wanted him to do, or because something else is wrong. Then I try to analyze my emotional responses.

Generally I avoid rewriting something unless I have an emotional response to it.

When you rewrite your own material, do you find it difficult to step back and take an objective view?

TOWNE: When I get involved in the reworking of something, I have several close friends on whose judgment I rely. I don't know if it's true of any other kind of writing, but screenwriting has two levels. One is when you're initially working on the script, doing it in isolation, away from all the mechanics of the making of the movie, the presence of the actors, the production problems. Then you finish and bring it into the real world, the real-phony world which is the movie world. That's a whole different process, and I think you've got to be schizophrenic about it. At one point you're more or less the creator, and then you're part of the group of people who are trying to bring something to life. It's difficult to make the distinction sometimes, but not all that difficult if you're working with people you trust and really care for. Then it can be very exciting.

You don't find that talking over the screenplay with others dissipates it for you?

TOWNE: There comes a point where you're confused, you don't know where you're going. Then it helps to talk. It was really true of *Chinatown*. I got lost so many times.

Do you see a preference among screenwriters for doing adaptations instead of original scripts?

TOWNE: I think it's a typical writer's problem: You'd rather work on somebody else's mediocre material than on your own mediocre material. In a strange way, it releases your writing abilities because you feel you don't have to take full responsibility for it. You might actually do better work because you're not stopping and worrying that it's you personally. And you learn things you don't learn doing your own material. So I have mixed feelings about it. I think it takes more courage, more stupidity—whatever you want to call it—to deal with original material.

In your adaptation of Darryl Ponicsan's The Last Detail, *you made an interesting change. Ponicsan kills off Billy Buddusky [played in the film by Jack Nicholson] at the end. You don't. Why not?*

TOWNE: In the novel, the character of Buddusky was an intellectual. He secretly read Camus. He also had a beautiful wife in New York. He was a very atypical sailor who had a kind of Whitmanesque appreciation of the sea. I wanted to tell a story about typical people, not atypical people. Without saying it or trying to be pushy about it, I wanted to imply that we're all lifers in the navy, and that we will go along and be helpful to someone if our kindness or our courtesy doesn't cost us too much and if it flatters our vanity [Buddusky and another sailor are detailed to escort a young sailor to the brig; along the way they attempt to educate him about life]. We'll get this kid laid, we'll buy him a few beers, we'll let him have a good time if that makes him think more of us, but we won't risk our neck. And all we'll do is feel a little guilty and cover it up by saying, "I hate this chicken-shit detail."

But people always hide behind their jobs when they have to do something unpleasant. Those on the detail were no better than they ought to be, and no worse. But they were not particularly courageous. Nobody is. I thought it would be dishonest to let the sailor off or to have the others feel so bad they would go AWOL or get themselves killed. I also thought this would let the audience off the hook. "Gee, we're not so bad. We let the guy go."

Earlier you indicated that the strong language is central to the movie. Why?

TOWNE: All the socially taboo language was necessary. From the time Rhett Butler said "Frankly, my dear, I don't give a damn" in *Gone with the Wind*, it has usually been the case that socially taboo language in film was for dramatic emphasis. But in *The Last Detail*, it was used for exactly the opposite reasons. In the service you swear a lot precisely because you are impotent. When Columbia said that wouldn't it be better to have twenty "motherfuckers" instead of forty "motherfuckers," I said no, because then you'd lose the point that these men can't do anything more than swear. The repetitiousness is an index of their inability to do anything else.

Did you have Jack Nicholson in mind when you wrote the screenplay?

TOWNE: Yes. I love to write for him. But Jack is a unique case for me because we've known each other for so long. Jack and I were in acting class together years ago—Jeff Corey's—and I saw him work two or three times a week for several years. I got to know him extremely well.

I've never really talked with François Truffaut, but I'd be willing to bet that he would not have written *Stolen Kisses*, he would not have written *The 400 Blows*, he would not have written some of his movies in the way he wrote them unless he knew that Jean-Pierre Léaud was alive and walking around. Léaud was his collaborator whether the actor knew it at the moment or not. Really good actors are your collaborators.

Was Shampoo *an original idea?*

TOWNE: Yes and no. Warren Beatty and I were talking one day about what would be a current adaptation of *The Country Wife*, Wycherley's Restoration comedy. It's a wonderful play about a man called Horner who lets it be known throughout all of social London that his doctor, Doctor Quack, has rendered him a eunuch. Consequently, all the husbands trust Horner with their wives, which is a big mistake. He's in fine shape. We talked about it, and Warren said, "Well, what would be the contemporary equivalent? An actor?" I said, "No, it would be a hairdresser."

You must know a fascinating hairdresser somewhere.

TOWNE: I was going with a woman who had been married to a hairdresser. I found out about it after we had been going together for about three months, and I was shocked and intrigued.

They are in an incredible position to cuckold a lot of men.

TOWNE: Yes. They are crude Pygmalions: they make women pretty. They know what their flaws are, or the women think they do, and they cover them up. And they touch them. For a lot of women—I don't mean just young, attractive women—maybe it's the most tender and intimate contact they have with anybody.

But Shampoo *doesn't really explore the idea of the hairdresser people think to be gay but isn't.*

TOWNE: *The Country Wife* idea never really developed. As I wrote, I realized there were other concerns. The only echo of it is in the hairdresser's relationship with Jack Warden and in the steamroom scene. It would have been a mistake to construct a movie just repeating that gag. But *Shampoo*, instead, is sort of *Our Town*. It's Grover's Corners 1968, only it's Beverly Hills. I'm genuinely fond of all the characters. I hope this was communicated to the audience.

When did you write Shampoo?

TOWNE: I did an early draft in 1970. Warren and I had some arguments over the script. He wanted to have one strong woman's role for Julie Christie, and I ended up writing two strong women's roles, or two roughly equivalent women's roles. His view was that neither role was strong or good. He was very angry about it, and I was very angry about his being angry about it, because I thought the script was really pretty terrific. For a period of about six months we hardly spoke, and the project was put aside for several years. Then he fitfully talked of reviving it and of adding the political element to the film. One of his major contributions, by the way, was to add the election part to the 1970 draft [the film takes place on the day, night, and morning after the 1968 presidential election].

He rewrote it?

TOWNE: He restructured some of the script and added the party sequences. Then in about eight days at the Beverly Wilshire Hotel [where Beatty was then living] I completely rewrote it with him and Hal Ashby. We'd argue about certain scenes, especially as time became an important factor. Warren is the kind of person who, once he makes up his mind to do something, after procrastinating seemingly forever, is hysterically committed to it.

What was the purpose, in your mind, of the scene near the end of Shampoo *when Warren Beatty returns to the beauty parlor and finds that the son of the older hairdresser has just been killed in an auto accident?*

TOWNE: Beatty's character has been getting away with everything; nothing seems to matter. He seems to be invulnerable, the feeling youth has that they can't possibly be hurt. He has gotten away with some dangerous things, not quite believing it. He walks into a beauty shop, which itself is unreal, and he hears that somebody has just died. People do die—it's something one tends to forget. It scares him; it makes him feel, "I'm going to die too. I want something before that happens." He's a guy who, without quite being aware of it, is undergoing a sort of breakdown. It's just more of the same, but it's more and more frenetic, and it gets out of hand: "God, this is fun . . . God, it's fun . . . God, it's not so much fun."

How did you get started writing for films?

TOWNE: I started writing professionally when I was in Jeff Corey's acting class. It was a peculiar class at that time because there were not only actors there; there were directors, producers, and writers. Among others there was Roger Corman. One day he said, "Kid, how'd you like to write a movie?" I said, "Fine." Roger would let anybody do anything no matter how badly you did it. Everyone I know—Jack Nicholson, Francis Coppola, I mean everybody—got started with Roger. He paid me about fifty cents for the first thing I wrote [*The Last Woman on Earth*, 1960, which Corman directed]. He figured it was worth it to see what somebody could come up with; it was a good gamble for him.

Was anything particularly helpful to you in learning the craft?

TOWNE: Yes. Seeing something done exactly the way it was written. It might not necessarily be good, but it was a great lesson either way. One of the hardest things about working in television was that everything got changed so much. You could never tell when something was bad, if it was you or if it was the fact that it had been changed. On *Bonnie and Clyde,* no matter how many times I was forced to rewrite, finally when it was agreed upon, it was shot exactly that way. I was able to gauge what I thought it would play like and then see what it actually played like in dailies. That was of immeasurable value to me.

When you write a screenplay, how much do you think in visual terms?

TOWNE: Generally speaking, the process of writing a screenplay is figuring out how to keep the dialogue as spare as possible. You think in terms of trying to advance the narrative not as much with dialogue as with image. Even if the narrative is being advanced while the people are talking, they should not be talking about the narrative.

Do you work on a day-to-day schedule?

TOWNE: I'm very undisciplined. I'm either working or I'm not working. I'm not somebody who is able to work three or four hours at a time, and then get up and go about my business. I couldn't do it. I have to get to the point where it's a matter of sheer desperation that something be finished, and then I work until I can't work any more, stop working, and then go back at it. *Do you organize a first draft or do you just wing it until you've got something on paper?*

TOWNE: You can't wing it. In the case of *Chinatown*, I was constantly trying to organize it. I wrote at least twenty different step outlines—long, long step outlines. Usually I have a pretty clear idea of where the screenplay is going, even if I don't know every step of the way.

Do you divide your step outline into three acts? Do you try to write a well-made play?

TOWNE: No. I try to see that it goes *some*where. I believe in soft openings for movies, anyway, which tends to throw out any conventional one-two-three arrangement.

Why do you have a preference for soft openings?

TOWNE: I think it's almost impossible to lose an audience in the first ten minutes, but almost inevitable in the last if you haven't laid the groundwork of the film at the beginning. It's not television. You don't have to grab them. In a movie with a very fast opening, you end up paying for it somewhere along the way—usually by having to explain what happened in the fast and furious action. I almost like it when a movie's a little boring in the beginning because it establishes a kind of credibility that you can build on. It's a ballast if you're going to do more and more implausible things and lead an audience down the garden path.

When you're writing, do you think of the audience—for example, in the tensions you're setting up?

TOWNE: What I think of most when I think of the audience is, "Will they understand this?" Tensions? What I try to deal with is what amuses, frightens *me*. The idea of a knife up the nose I found very scary. I don't think, "This will scare the audience." It was something that would bother *me*.

Are the production problems in your mind as you're working?

TOWNE: The closer you get to production the more they are in front of your mind. Also, things change a lot when you're rewriting and when the actors are suddenly there. It's unpredictable what happens then because the script is no longer fiction. No matter how hard you worked in isolation, suddenly you're dealing with real people, the actors, who are liable to know moment to moment what their characters are going to do, what they're going to be like, better than you. They'll also know it's going to be their faces up there, and they don't want to look like schmucks. They're going to know better than anyone if there's something awkward or inconsistent.

What's the attitude of the industry toward screenwriters? Has there been a change lately?

TOWNE: I can only speak for myself, but I feel I'm respected and listened to, at this point. I'm included in the process of the making of the movie, but I ask to be included. The writer can be another eye on the set. You're obliged to be supportive of the director as much as possible, because he's in a highly vulnerable position, but that doesn't mean agreeing with him all the time. It means clashing when you feel it's essential and trying to guide him where you feel it is useful to him. You hope he'll do the same for you.

It can be as much the fault of writers as it is of insecure directors that writers are not on the set. I think not to be on the set is an abdication of your responsibility. Some screenwriters are not willing to submit themselves or their work to the exacerbating day-by-day process of the making of a movie. It's humiliating. Each moment committed to paper must be challenged. The screenplay is just a blueprint. It's a fantasy. No matter how good a script is, it's going to be rewritten. In this, movies are unlike plays. In a play you rehearse, and then you perform. As you shoot a movie, it's a combination of rehearsal and performance.

When you're writing, are you aware of the combination?

TOWNE: Yes. A movie is not quite performance level, and it's not quite rehearsal level. It's a Never-Never Land you're in, and because of the peculiar financial and temporal demands of moviemaking, it's necessary that you rework, improvise, take what the actors give you on a moment-to-moment basis and exploit it. The great directors are exploiters. The great director is a person who can see what's going on at the time and can capitalize on it. And he needs all the help he can get, whether it comes from a writer or a grip.

In this sense, then, a playwright can be the sole author of a play, but the screenwriter can't really be the sole author of a movie?

TOWNE: Nobody can be the sole author of a movie. Not even the director. Ideally, a movie should be one man's vision or it should be a mutually agreed upon vision which everyone helps to achieve. The execution is what to quarrel over. The only thing important is that somebody cares enough to see it steadily and whole, as they used to say about life.

What steps can a young screenwriter take to ensure that his script remains intact?

TOWNE: I don't think you can, unless you are fortunate enough to work together from the beginning with a friend who is a director and it becomes a communal effort. If you're not interested in directing, find someone you like and respect and try to put it together that way. Look to your peers, your contemporaries. Find friends you love talking with about film, whom you like working with, who stimulate you, so that you more or less agree from the beginning.

As Hollywood rates power, knowing people like Warren Beatty and Jack Nicholson gives you a certain amount of power in getting something made, doesn't it?

TOWNE: No. Commercial success is what gives you power. Everybody meets everybody, but part of the reason you continue to know people is because you've worked with them, and it's gone well. Your friends almost inevitably become the people with whom you work. When you're young, you can be friendly with a lot of people in different professions. As you get older, it gets harder and harder because you get more and more focused. Even my contacts with my close friends now come down to business discussions. I sometimes think I won't be friends with my friends, as it would be good to be, until we get old.

Did you work on the set of Chinatown, *and to what degree were you involved in the actual production after finishing your final draft?*

TOWNE: I was with *Chinatown* until about a week before shooting started, and then I was given to understand I would not be welcome on the set, which, under the circumstances, I think was wise of Roman. At that time Roman and I would have had a hard time agreeing on the color of Faye's nail polish. But I followed it with the rushes [the daily screening of unedited footage], and then I was with the post-production. On *Shampoo*, I was never off the set. But I have an unusual relationship with both Hal

Ashby and Warren Beatty. They'd actually have me crouching under the camera—it's difficult for some people to allow that. I once worked for a week and a half with Philippe de Broca, who directed *The Joker, King of Hearts,* and *That Man from Rio.* We were working on a pirate movie. He was more fun to work with than anybody I'd worked with before—stimulating, exciting. He really had what is called Gallic charm. I remember coming up with an idea, and he said, "Oh, Bobby, that is just great, but you must allow me to think I thought of it myself."

Directing is the hardest work in the world. Some directors can't abide the sight of someone who might be involved at a very elemental level in the creation of something. Others are much more mature or shrewd about it and invite collaboration and exploit it. Francis Coppola, for example, is wonderful in his ability to have his own vision and at the same time be malleable. You never feel he doesn't have any idea of what he wants, yet he's able to take from other people who have something to offer. But there are others who are so threatened by ideas or suggestions that they tend to want to shut them off. It's one of the reasons why it's valuable to have close relations with the people you work with. Any conflict which comes up is not necessarily viewed as disrespect or as questioning of the other's talent. You're people who care about each other and who are going for a common goal. It's really good to work with your friends.

THE ACTOR
Charlton Heston

Charlton Heston was once described by a French critic as "an axiom of the cinema." Weathering changes of fashion, Heston's heroic screen image has remained a bulwark of Hollywood for more than thirty years.

Heston is best known for his portrayal of epic and historical figures in such films as *Ben-Hur* (for which he won an Oscar), *The Ten Commandments, El Cid, 55 Days at Peking, The Agony and the Ecstasy,* and *The Greatest Story Ever Told.* He has also been the anchor of such varied commercial successes as *The Greatest Show on Earth, Planet of the Apes,* and *Earthquake.*

But he has always been restless with the limitations of his image, and has attempted to broaden it and take chances with more offbeat roles. His saddle tramp in *Will Penny* and his visionary British general, "Chinese" Gordon, in *Khartoum* are among his finest achievements as an actor. Heston also won critical praise for his work in Orson Welles's *Touch of Evil* and Richard Lester's *The Three Musketeers,* and he has made films of Shakespeare's *Julius Caesar* (twice) and *Antony and Cleopatra,* as well as frequently appearing in Shakespeare plays on stage.

Born John Charlton Carter in 1924, he was raised in Michi-

83

gan and Illinois and attended acting school at Northwestern University. He appeared on daytime radio drama in Chicago and starred in two 16-millimeter amateur films, *Peer Gynt* (1941) and *Julius Caesar* (1949), directed by fellow Northwestern student David Bradley.

After World War II service, Heston went to New York seeking work as a stage actor, without much success. His break came on live television, appearing in such programs as *Wuthering Heights, Of Human Bondage, Macbeth,* and *Jane Eyre,* and the latter won him a Hollywood contract from producer Hal Wallis.

Heston's first professional film was *Dark City* (1950), but it took Cecil B. DeMille to make him a star by casting him in the lead role of the circus manager in *The Greatest Show on Earth,* which won the Oscar for best picture of 1952. During the 1950s and 1960s Heston appeared in many epics, Westerns, and other costume sagas.

In the 1970s he was a familiar figure in the disaster-film and science-fiction cycles, proving his adaptability to commercial vicissitudes. During that period he also made his film directing debut with *Antony and Cleopatra,* and made frequent stage appearances in Los Angeles.

Heston has been highly active in service to the film industry and the U.S. government. He was president of the Screen Actors Guild for six terms and has been involved with the American Film Institute since its inception in 1967, serving as both chairman of the Board of Trustees and currently as board president. He has been a board member of the National Council on the Arts, a member of the Presidential Task Force for the Arts and Humanities, and has made many appearances around the world on behalf of the U.S. State Department. In 1980 he published a memoir, *The Actor's Life: Journals 1956–1976.*

FILMOGRAPHY

1941 *Peer Gynt*   1949 *Julius Caesar*   1950 *Dark City*   1952 *The Greatest Show on Earth* / *The Savage* / *Ruby Gentry*   1953 *Pony Express* / *The President's Lady* / *Arrowhead* / *Bad for Each Other*   1954 *The Naked Jungle* / *Secret of the Incas*   1955

The Far Horizons | The Private War of Major Benson | Lucy Gallant 1956 *The Ten Commandments* 1957 *Three Violent People* 1958 *Touch of Evil | The Big Country | The Buccaneer* 1959 *Ben-Hur | The Wreck of the Mary Deare* 1961 *El Cid* 1962 *The Pigeon That Took Rome | Diamond Head* 1963 *55 Days at Peking* 1965 *The Greatest Story Ever Told | Major Dundee | The Agony and the Ecstasy | The War Lord* 1966 *Khartoum* 1967 *Counterpoint* 1968 *Planet of the Apes | Will Penny* 1969 *Number One* 1970 *Beneath the Planet of the Apes | The Hawaiians | Julius Caesar* 1971 *The Omega Man* 1972 *Antony and Cleopatra* (also director) *| Skyjacked* 1973 *Call of the Wild | Soylent Green* 1974 *The Three Musketeers | Airport '75 | Earthquake* 1975 *The Four Musketeers* 1976 *Midway | The Last Hard Man | Two-Minute Warning* 1977 *The Prince and the Pauper (Crossed Swords)* 1978 *Gray Lady Down* 1980 *The Mountain Men | The Awakening* 1982 *Mother Lode* (also director)

THE SEMINAR

Charlton Heston held seminars with the Fellows of the Center for Advanced Film Studies on October 28, 1970; January 20, 1976; July 27, 1977; and November 14, 1979.

What qualities does an actor look for in a director?
HESTON: Above all, a director has to be a good captain. We're committed to democracy, in this country at least, but I promise you, a movie location is not a democracy. Many people have observed the remarkable parallels between filmmaking and a military operation—the problems of logistics, personnel, communication, transportation, food, morale, weather, and luck are all the same. So is the need for leadership. This is not the only ingredient; obviously, talent, intelligence, imagination, and physical energy are vital prerequisites for a director, but I've come to feel that the quality of captaincy is crucial among these.

That doesn't mean being a screaming tyrant. You don't *demand* obedience, you evoke it. Franklin Schaffner is one of the best captains in my experience—Frank directed me in *Macbeth* and half a dozen pieces for live television, and I've done two pictures [*The War Lord*, 1965, and *Planet of the Apes*, 1968] with him. Frank is the eye of the storm. He is a totally calm man, able to command without ever raising his voice; he comes on the set knowing exactly what he wants to do. I always like to feel I know more about the scene than the director does, but I never quite feel that with Frank. I always feel that he's read it one more time than I have. He gets up at five in the morning when he's shooting, and he has scale models of all his sets and toy soldiers for the characters. He plans all his moves, then comes on the set and tells you what he wants. Obviously, a lot of the time it doesn't work out that way. Considering the meticulous nature of his preparation, it's remarkable the degree of flexibility he allows himself on the set. That gives him the best of both worlds. He looks for the absolute utmost his preparation can arrive at, but he's able to keep himself open for creative developments during shooting. That's a good captain.

To look at the question from the other side, what do you see as your relationship with the director?
HESTON: I came to realize very early in films that the actor is the servant of the camera. The camera is what tells the story, and the actor, in a sense, is merely the most important prop. The butterfly on a dead man's hand at the end of *All Quiet on the Western Front* [directed by Lewis Milestone, 1931] is a far more eloquent image than anything the best actor who ever drew breath could give you there.

That's one of the reasons I still keep my passport valid on the stage, because that's actor's country. On the stage, the whole thing is the play, and the actor is the vehicle that communicates it to the audience. No matter how talented a stage director is, no matter how much he may give you, on opening night he goes across the street and gets smashed and you're up there by yourself. You own the stage, and the play.

Film is different. No matter how much I know about a film, no matter how crucial I may have been in putting it together—I may have found the property and been deeply involved in shaping the script before the director even came on it—finally, once I approve a director, I must surrender a large part of the control to him; really *all* the control, I think. I call directors "sir," even though I'm now at a point where at least half of them are younger than I am. Film is primarily a director's medium, and many very successful and effective film actors are not actors at all in the professional sense. Conversely, many a fine stage actor lacks the elusive, indefinable chemistry that makes the camera love him.

Bearing in mind that different films and characters create different problems for the actor, do you have any general principles you have followed in your career?
HESTON: If you want me to tell you all about acting, you missed a golden opportunity: the time I could tell you all about acting was when I was studying at Northwestern. Since then I've discovered more and more about which I know less and less. When you're studying acting, you think anybody who doesn't work the way you're taught is violating the true faith, but the longer I've acted, the more I've come to believe in a catholic—with a small

"c"—approach to acting. Finally you realize that it's not so much a question of dogma—in acting all that matters is that it works. I've found that you can do your best work under a startling variety of directorial approaches. I've worked with directors who like to improvise, I've worked with directors who like to rehearse, I've worked with directors who like to come in with the moves all previously plotted. It's surprising how easy it is to adapt.

In terms of how you work, which was your question, you work the way the director wants to work. I believe you are professionally required to adapt yourself. I say to directors with whom I haven't worked before, "Look, I have a loud second-balcony voice and very strong opinions. I've been involved with the project a long time, and I'll tell you what I think. But if we differ and you can't persuade me, or get tired of trying to, just say, 'Chuck, do it my way because that's the way I want you to do it.'" Actors who are anxious about surrendering their concept are often insecure. The more secure the actor is, the more likely he is to recognize that there is really more than one way to do it. The director is the only one who has a concept of the whole film. Every night at three A.M. the film is run in the projection room inside his skull. That's why directors come in looking so tired in the morning. Nobody else knows what footage is exposed there. That's why in film you have to surrender yourself far more to the director.

Could we talk about some of the other directors you've worked with—Sam Peckinpah, for instance?

HESTON: An enormously gifted man. Not a good captain. I worked for Sam on a picture whose wounds still bleed because I keep picking at 'em. *Major Dundee* [1965] is, in my judgment, a painful failure, with some fascinating things in it, but structurally almost a total disaster. There has never been a film that really began to explore the significance of the Civil War as one of the watershed American experiences, and that's what I had in mind with *Major Dundee*. What Sam had in mind was, I think, *The Wild Bunch* [the landmark Western Peckinpah made four years later], and what the studio had in mind was a film that made a lot of money and was about cowboys and Indians.

I'd like to make another picture for Sam, but it's awfully tough to work with him. You need to make an enormously strong personal commitment to Sam. That means you have to sit up all night with him in those Mexican bars and drink that absolutely foul Mexican brandy. And you have to *discuss* things all the time—not just the script, but the world and *everything*. And you have to sit up talking to the guys in the silk suits [the studio executives], and then you've got to spend half an hour telling one another how terrible *They* are, with a capital "T." There are directors who seem to function well in an atmosphere of continuing crisis. Sam is one. Personally, I can't stand it.

I had as close a relationship with Sam on that picture as I've ever had with a director. I think one of the best things in the picture is the character, and I can say that without immodesty, because to a greater degree than in most of my films it was an involuntary creation. Sam *made* me into Major Dundee, drinking in those cantinas. I guess he directed me as much in there as he did on the set, maybe unconsciously. Also, there was something about sitting on a horse all day in a Union cavalryman's pants that made the people seem like horse soldiers, not actors, and this was part of Sam's contribution to the film.

The first time in years that I tried to do someone serious bodily harm was to Sam Peckinpah. I consider myself a remarkably tolerant and patient sort of fellow. If you can go through two pictures with William Wyler, you can survive anything. But at the end of a very tough day, I tried to ride Sam down with a cavalry sabre.

The question was whether he had directed me to lead a cavalry troop down a mountain slope at a trot or at a canter. He said we'd come down too slowly and I replied, "Sam, you told me to come at a trot. If you would like me to lead them at a canter, I will lead them at a canter, but *you said trot*." And he said, "No, goddamn it, you dumb bastard, I told you to canter!" That did it. I was on this big black stud, about sixty yards away from him, and I wheeled and charged him, at a full gallop, sabre in hand. He was, fortunately, standing next to the Chapman boom [a camera crane], which had a sixty-foot neck. He scrambled aboard and signaled it up out of my reach, which they barely succeeded in doing before I got there. I regained my shattered cool, led the troop up the slope and back down, at a canter. Somewhat white-faced, Sam said, "Print," and I said, "Thank you."

How was it working with Orson Welles on Touch of Evil *[1958]?*
HESTON: Orson is the most talented man I've ever worked
with, and I found him the most exciting director I ever worked
for. His talent is so abundant and fertile that I think it sometimes
does him a disservice. Things come so easily to him and he can
think of so many fruitful solutions to directing problems that he
perhaps doesn't find which is the best because they are all so
much better than what anyone else would think up. I don't know
whether it's more Orson's tragedy or film's tragedy that his career
has been so crippled by his now forty-year conflict with the movie
industry. He's an extremely complicated, utterly charming, unpredictable, and in some respects I'm afraid I'd have to say un-
reliable man. But I learned more from him about acting and
about filmmaking than from any other director.

I've never worked with a director who communicated better
with actors. He is himself an actor of considerable ability, and he
can tell you things about the scene and routes to solve it that you
never thought of; this is all peppered with terribly funny anecdotes about the Mercury Theater [the stage company Welles and
John Houseman ran in New York in the late 1930s] or something he said to [director] Carol Reed on *The Third Man,* or
something that happened with Marlene Dietrich in a bar in Paris,
or some funny dirty story you never heard about Harry Cohn
[head of Columbia Pictures until his death in 1958]. It's a formidable performance in itself, and in the course of it he inspires
you. His directions about acting are quite pragmatic. I remember
he said something that impressed me enormously: "Very few leading men understand the importance of the tenor range." The
more I thought about that, the more I realized it's true, and I
have since attempted to explore this truth to my profit. British
officers in the nineteenth century were taught at Sandhurst to use
what they called "the tenor of command," because a tenor voice
carries more penetratingly than a bass or baritone, especially when
giving commands. I was able to raise my voice largely into a tenor
range to play General Charles "Chinese" Gordon in *Khartoum*
[directed by Basil Dearden, 1966]. I probably wouldn't have
thought of that or wouldn't have been able to do it if ten years
before Orson hadn't made that singular observation. That's not
the kind of comment a director is likely to make to you, but it's

terribly useful. Orson can think of ten ways to tell you something if you don't get it the way he tells you the first time.

The way we got into *Touch of Evil* was interesting. I can't resist boasting about how it happened, because it may be, in the end, one of my most significant contributions to film. The script was submitted to me by Universal; it was a fairly routine police thriller. I said, "It's all right. But because the formula has been explored so many times, this picture depends more than most on who's going to direct it." They said, "We don't know yet, but Orson Welles is going to play the heavy." And I said, "Well, he's a pretty good director—why don't you have him direct it?" This seemed to strike them as a staggeringly radical suggestion, as though I'd suggested my mother direct the picture. They said, "We'll get back to you." I was amazed. This was the man who made *Citizen Kane* and *The Magnificent Ambersons* and *The Lady from Shanghai*. They got back, finally, and said, "OK, we'll have Orson direct it." I knew he'd rewrite the script totally, which he did, in a week.

At least one or two shots in the picture have become legends: the boom shot that opens the film certainly is among them. It's an incredible shot [following Heston and Janet Leigh for several blocks until a concealed bomb blows up a passing car]; it took us all night to make. But I think an equally interesting shot is the scene in which Quinlan [the police captain played by Welles] interrogates the suspect in his apartment, and Joe Calleia [playing Quinlan's deputy] "finds" the dynamite planted by Quinlan as the incriminating evidence. The scene was thirteen pages, and it was scheduled for the first three days' shooting on the picture. The weekend before we started, on both Saturday and Sunday, the principals rehearsed the scene at Orson's house, when he mostly worked out the camera positions. This had a very clear purpose—to him. It wasn't clear to us until he shot it.

I've rehearsed ahead of production with four directors: Welles, Laurence Olivier, Wyler, and Peckinpah. The only ones who seemed to me to use the rehearsal time constructively were Welles and Olivier, both of whom, of course, are theater people. With Wyler and Peckinpah, we had a lot of fun and told stories and drank coffee, but we really didn't get a lot done. With Orson we got a hell of a lot done.

He worked meticulously with the camera all Monday morning on what it soon became clear was a master shot encompassing the whole scene. It was really very tricky. Aside from being thirteen pages long, the scene had four or five speaking roles and a couple of extras coming in, and an insert of the dynamite, as well as action in three rooms. It was an unusual scene to consider doing in one setup, but Orson was determined to get it. We went through the entire morning and never turned a camera.

After lunch, the executives began to arrive on the set, though they never quite summoned up the nerve to approach Orson directly. They were nervous about him; this was the first picture Welles had made in an American studio in eleven years. They huddled about in uneasy little groups in the shadows, shaking their heads. We never rolled a camera until ten minutes after five. Of course, it was difficult and things went wrong. Finally we got a print at six-fifteen, and Orson said, "OK. Cut. Print. That's a wrap on this set. I'm through with this scene. We're two days ahead of schedule."

This shocked the executives, who'd been practically prostrate with gloom, and carried them to heights of euphoria and visions of a ten-day schedule. Of course, he was throwing them a curve by demonstrating how fast he could work. The only reason he did that shot in one setup was to establish control over the picture. They always thought, "Gee, maybe he's going to get thirteen pages in one day again." He never *did*, but they always thought he *might*. One of the reasons I tell this story is that Orson has an undeserved reputation for being a wildly extragavant and irresponsible director. The film was budgeted at $880,000 and came in at $1.04 million; it was scheduled for twenty-eight shooting days and came in at thirty-one; both are effective refutations of that charge. It's true that Orson doesn't relate well to the studio executives who finally control his destiny, but there are directors of far less talent who have gone over budget more on *one film* than Orson has spent in all the films he's made in his career.

More than any other director I've worked for, Orson could somehow persuade you that every setup you did was the most important setup in the picture. A great many scenes you do in films are not very interesting. If you're doing a shot of someone driving up, parking, and going upstairs, it's indeed possible to think of some fascinating things to do with the camera, or with the cutting, but it's hard to make it interesting for the actor. Orson can persuade you it's the most important shot in the picture. He can ignite a company's enthusiasm, not only the actors, but everyone— the guy who sweeps the stage. Grips and electricians tend to be pretty blasé about filmmaking, but on his pictures they're not. I can't overstress the value of this ability.

You mentioned that you managed to "survive" working with William Wyler. What did you mean by that?

HESTON: Doing a picture for Wyler is like getting the works in a Turkish bath—you damn near drown, but you come out smelling like a rose. Willy is one of the best directors I've worked for, one of the best I've ever seen. He is a *terrible* communicator, but his sense of the rightness of a scene is so perfect, and, above all, his infallible sense of performance, coupled with his list of credits, gives him the authority to bring it off. Personally he is charming, but when he is working he is relentless.

He would come in and say, "Eight o'clock in the morning is a hell of a time to play a love scene. Let's have some coffee. And let's get some light in the set—it looks like a set. Let's make it look like a room." So they'd light it, and he'd say, "Well, all right, I guess you have to come in." Mind you, he had thought about the scene a great deal. But more than any other director I worked for, he was able to postpone the final creative choice. He'd shoot three, seven, nine, eleven takes on a scene and then say, "Why are you being so harsh?" You'd say, "You told me I was supposed to get angry at her." He'd say, "That was a terrible idea. I shouldn't have told you that." It takes great security to do that. Then he'd say, "OK, that's pretty good. But it's not very spontaneous." You'd say, "Well, Jesus, Willy, we've been putting stuff in and taking stuff out for two hours. How *can* it be?" He'd say, "I don't know, but it *has* to be." So you'd keep fiddling with it, and finally all you'd get would be, "OK, let's do her close-up now."

When he printed a take, it was as good as you could do it. He knew when it was right. But he was like a watchmaker taking a watch apart and putting it together, ignoring the fact that it's not a watch, it's a human being. I remember when I was working for him the first time, in *The Big Country* [1958]. After we'd spent an hour and a half on a very short close-up, he said, "All right, let's do the dolly shot." I said, "Willy, let's not give up now. I'll get it. Just tell me what to do." He said, "Chuck, if I don't say anything, that means it's OK." On *Ben-Hur* [1959], we were seven months into the shooting, and it was a cold, rainy November day. We'd finished shooting a rough eleven-hour day, the kind Willy always shot. I was waiting for my car in the rain, and Willy walked by. "Goodnight, Chuck," he said. "You were good today." I was dumbfounded. *"What?"* "The *scene*," Willy said, "you were very good in it." "Oh," I said. "Thanks. Thanks very much." That was the only time, on two pictures.

I think he didn't put much faith in acting as an art or actors as artists. He just knew how to use them to get what he wanted. And it may also be that he knew his man: I work well when I'm pressed. I like to feel that I'm being pushed absolutely as far as I can go, and I feel uneasy with directors who say, "Oh, that's fabulous." You think, "Fabulous? How can it be fabulous?" Once after we had looked at dailies, Willy said, "Have you ever noticed how often the dailies are marvelous and the pictures are lousy?" Which, of course, is true.

I'll tell you what he made me realize, and it's a useful lesson for an actor and certainly for a director. *You can always do it better.* Of course, you're compromising every second—all artists compromise their creative vision with their human limitations, and filmmakers have to add to that the compromises imposed on them by the enormous costs of the raw material they work with. You know you're going to have to finish the scene before lunch because you have to cross the stream by two P.M. or the light will go, and tomorrow a hundred and fifty horses are coming. It's all very well for a director to say, "Nobody's going to make me do anything less than the best I can." That's marvelous, but if you run four months over schedule they may not give you any more electric trains to play with. You *have* to compromise, just as Michelangelo did when he painted the ceiling, and for some of the same reasons. Still, as I learned from Willy, you can always get it a little better.

Over the years you have developed a very strong, well-defined image as an actor. People think of Charlton Heston as a next-door neighbor to God. Do you look for roles that go against the grain, to test your image?

HESTON: Every actor has to deal with the fact that, as his career continues, he is followed by the lengthening shadow of all the roles in which the audience remembers him. Their perception of those roles colors how they see him in the other parts he does. I've been more fortunate than some of my colleagues in getting a wider range of parts; I guess I'm one of the few American actors who do other nationalities. I do more biographical parts than most of my contemporaries, and I do a great many period parts.

I was never a juvenile. When I was twenty years old, I nearly starved to death. I was too big and my voice was too heavy and I had this broken nose. It was fortunate that early in my career I began to put on false noses and wigs and funny clothes and write with feathers. By now a French audience will accept me as a six-teenth-century French cardinal, a Mexican audience will accept me as a twentieth-century Mexican lawyer, an English audience will accept me as a Tudor king, and so on. I fight to get that elbow room.

I've been very fortunate in having had the experience through some fifty films of playing so many extraordinary men. I believe in the extraordinary man. The chance I've had to scrape around inside the skulls of men like Andrew Jackson, Michelangelo, Gordon, Mark Anthony, Cardinal Richelieu, Henry VIII, and Macbeth has been an enriching experience for me. To play them is a problem, because we live in a time that tends to reject the concept of the extraordinary man. We're fond of saying that we live in the century of the common man; our time is oriented toward the individual as victim. I've played a couple of victims—Will Penny [in the film of that name, directed by Tom Gries, 1967], I suppose, is a victim; Vargas in *Touch of Evil* is a victim—but by and large my physical equipment doesn't make me likely casting for parts like that.

The whole idea of the genuinely great man is out of currency. I reject that. I believe the significant work of the world has been done by the extraordinary individuals that this species produces every so often. I remember when I was researching Thomas Jefferson for a television film [*The Patriots*, 1963] I was struck by a description of him by a contemporary as "a man able to write a sonnet, break a horse, dance a minuet, run a surveying line, and tie an artery." I submit to you that none of us knows anybody who can do all of those things. Great men are marvelous to play. You feel a great inadequacy, sort of suspended inside this vast figure, straining desperately to fill it.

What kind of preparation do you do for a part?

HESTON: It depends on the kind of part. For a biographical role, you read all the biographies, and you've also got to read all the material you can on the period. The more remote it is, the more difficult it is to communicate to an audience. There are often physical preparations necessary—learning to drive the chariot in *Ben-Hur* is an example. I've played a couple of modern roles that also required physical preparation. I played a symphony conductor once [in *Counterpoint*, directed by Ralph Nelson, 1967], and learning to conduct, or to seem to conduct, a symphony took about two months. The longest preparation was for playing a professional football quarterback in *Number One* [directed by Tom Gries, 1968]. I played football in high school, but I was a receiver, and quarterbacking was like a whole new sport. To learn to make moves like a pro quarterback took eight months of concentrated effort on my part and very patient instruction on the part of the USC and New Orleans Saints coaching staffs.

I made a grievous mistake in preparing *Ben-Hur*: I wrote about twenty pages of background on the character of Ben-Hur—his boyhood, his family, his early friendship with Messala—and I showed it to Willy Wyler. He thought this was just the kind of show-off, actory thing that actors do, and that I was the biggest horse's ass he'd ever worked with. It took a month of shooting to get over it with me. Willy was suspicious of theory, but some other directors would have loved that.

When I did a film about the battle of Midway [*Midway*, directed by Jack Smight, 1977], most of the actors played real people, and I had the only principal role that was fictional. I was playing an air operations officer on the USS *Yorktown*. There were such men, of course, but they purposely structured a role that would be anonymous in history so they could give him a more complex personal story than you could with a real individual. I said to the technical advisor, a retired admiral who had been in the battle, "I want to be able to fit this guy in with all these real people. Henry Fonda is reading the biography of Ches-

ter Nimitz. Help me construct a career for this man I'm playing."
The admiral was intrigued. He said, "Your guy was a captain in
1941, which means he probably would have made commander in
the mid-'30s. Until about '35, they retired naval aviators at the
rank of commander, and to have survived that you'd have to
have been a hot-shot. I made you class of 1916 because a lot of
excellent officers came from that class. At that time, to go into
aviation training you would have had to do two years of sea duty
first, as a line officer. Let's see, that would still be during World
War I. We could put you as an ensign on a destroyer in the Atlan-
tic fleet, which was very good duty. You could have gotten some
citations. That would then mark you as a comer, so they wouldn't
retire you in the mid-'30s." Suddenly the guy's background began
to come alive for me. I had this typed up and kept it in my script.
Henry Fonda would be looking up stuff in his two-volume biography of Nimitz, and I would be looking at my little typewritten
list.

*What do you consider your best work in films, and what were the
factors that contributed to making it so?*
HESTON: I guess either *Will Penny* or Gordon. Both films had
beautifully written scripts. Robert Ardrey did the script for *Khartoum*; it's one of the best scripts I've ever read. That and Tom
Gries's script for *Will Penny* were about the only scripts I've ever
had in which almost nothing was changed on the set. And another factor was that both films were made in the real settings.
We shot *Will Penny* in the High Sierra, and if you're really chasing one lousy stray cow up among the jackpine above the snow-
line in January, you know how it feels to chase a lone cow in the
jackpine in 1885. We shot *Khartoum* in the Sudan, and the Nile
is the Nile. There you are, on the same river Gordon sailed up to
get his head chopped off.

What pleased me about Gordon was the acting challenge. If
Peter O'Toole had played Gordon, it wouldn't have been as hard
for him as it was for me; for an American actor to play a specific
nineteenth-century British hero presents a number of problems,
primarily in terms of accent and physical appearance, although
oddly enough I look a lot like him. In playing any real person, or
even a mythic person who is widely known, one of the problems
is that people have a preconceived idea of what he was like. It's

difficult for an actor to satisfy everybody's preconception. For an American audience, this was of no significance because most Americans have never heard of Gordon, but to British audiences he's as well known as Pershing is to us. The English liked the performance, so I guess I squeaked by with it.

Gordon was one of that curious maverick strain of soldier-mystics that England managed to produce every generation or so. He was an odd, thorny, interior person, perhaps a bit mad but quite extraordinary. I remember reading one of the contemporary accounts of Gordon: a Sudanese who had been around him a great deal said, "When Gordon Pasha looks at you, you feel that you cannot lie." I tried somehow to use that in the performance. And all the reading I did, which included several biographies and his letters, indicated that one of the things he was looking for most eagerly all his life was his own death, and that was one of the reasons for his remarkable, frightening physical courage. He was a deeply religious man, and saw his own death as a passage to a more important existence. That's why I played his death with a smile, and also because Gordon knew that the most important contribution he could make was to be killed in Khartoum. Everybody wanted him to come out—London *and* the Mahdi. The Mahdi knew perfectly well that killing Gordon was a terrible idea, but Gordon double-crossed them. He was a curious man.

I suppose one of the things that appealed to me about *Will Penny* was that it was a small picture. Most Westerns are about the mythic West and the extraordinary man. Will Penny was not such a man. I was interested in exploring an illiterate cowhand. Most men in the real West were not the fastest gun in Dodge City or the richest rancher on the Ponderosa; they were men who scraped out a terribly hard living with their hands and a horse, chasing cows. That most of them were constructive, largely optimistic men is a remarkable affirmation of the human spirit.

I found a marvelous line in one of the diaries of old cowboys that I read while preparing the picture. We wanted to use it, but we never found a place for it. After a particularly tough day, just a string of disasters—losing his hat, his stirrup breaking, cows getting drowned in a river, a guy breaking his leg—finally the cowboy wrote, "I guess you just gotta keep on keepin' on." That's all Will Penny does. He is extraordinary in only one particular, and it's the one which maybe more than any other is part of the American character: Will Penny was responsible. He wasn't particularly brave or bright or sensitive or anything else, but he was responsible. If he said he was going to do something, he did it. That's what the picture is about—that and his incapacity to live up to the final responsibility of a personal relationship.

Actors are dependent on the parts that are offered them, but I have been fortunate in having a lot of chances to explore the theme of responsibility, especially responsibility as experienced by the extraordinary man, which I've come to realize is a theme that interests me greatly.

Film is the art form of the twentieth century, and filmmakers naturally think of themselves as artists. The artist likes to feel that he has no responsibility other than to his own artistic integrity. I think the filmmaker has to assume a certain social responsibility as well. Certain of my colleagues would disagree with this, but I feel quite strongly about it.

When we made *Skyjacked* [directed by John Guillermin, 1972], the Federal Aviation Agency was very nervous about our doing it. I told the producer [Walter Seltzer] and the screenwriter [Stanley R. Greenberg], "Look, I don't know what kind of picture this is going to be, but I'll tell you one thing we're *not* going to do: we're not going to give anyone the idea that it's a good idea to hijack an airplane." And I don't think we did. The point of view of the picture is on the side of society, and I think that's important. I've turned down a number of pictures in the last few years that I might otherwise have taken because I think you have to be for society.

It's all very well to say, "I want to make an antiestablishment statement," but film is a terribly powerful tool. It's not like a painting or a poem or a novel or a newspaper article. Film crosses national boundaries, language barriers; it can even speak to people who can't read. It makes me nervous, it really does, to see pictures that are too strongly against *us*, because "us" is everybody. Films *can* change the world.

Bette Davis

A legendary actress who is still playing leading roles after more than fifty years in front of the camera, Bette Davis won the respect of both her directors and her audience for her independent spirit and her fierce devotion to truth.

Never a glamour girl, Davis fought for tougher roles and was not afraid of playing unsympathetic or villainous roles. As a result, she achieved a sharply defined screen image that gave her performances an enduring vitality and gave her career its remarkable longevity.

Born Ruth Elizabeth Davis in Lowell, Massachusetts, in 1908, she made her Broadway debut in a 1929 comedy, *Broken Dishes*. She was signed by Universal for her film debut in *Bad Sister* (1931), but the studio soon dropped her. George Arliss gave her career a critical boost by picking her for his leading lady in *The Man Who Played God* (1932), the first of her many films as a Warner Brothers contract player.

But it was a loan-out role for RKO, the cruel Mildred in the 1934 film of W. Somerset Maugham's *Of Human Bondage*, that established Davis as a major screen talent. Under contract to

Warners until 1942, she had frequent battles with the front office, gradually winning the complex roles she demanded to play.

After her first Oscar, for *Dangerous* (1935), she won another in her initial teaming with director William Wyler on *Jezebel* in 1938. They made two other notable films together, Maugham's *The Letter* and Lillian Hellman's *The Little Foxes*. Davis also achieved career highlights at Warners in two less distinguished properties, *Dark Victory* and *Now, Voyager*.

Her career faltered after she left the studio, but it soared briefly in 1950 with her portrayal of the aging actress Margo Channing in Joseph L. Mankiewicz's *All About Eve*, which remains her most celebrated role. Occasionally returning to the stage, in 1961 Davis created the role of Maxine Faulk in Tennessee Williams's play *The Night of the Iguana*. In the 1960s she had a new vogue in horror films, such as *What Ever Happened to Baby Jane?*; *Hush . . . Hush, Sweet Charlotte*; and *The Nanny*.

Her first TV movie was *Madame Sin* in 1972, and she has been much in demand on the home screen ever since. She has appeared in such well-received TV movies as *The Disappearance of Aimee, Family Reunion*, and *Little Gloria . . . Happy at Last*, and she received an Emmy for *Strangers: The Story of a Mother and Daughter* (1979).

Davis is a former president of the Academy of Motion Picture Arts and Sciences. In 1977 she became the first woman to receive The American Film Institute's Life Achievement Award. She published her autobiography *The Lonely Life*, in 1962.

SELECTED FILMOGRAPHY

1931 *Bad Sister* / *Waterloo Bridge*   1932 *The Man Who Played God* / *Cabin in the Cotton* / *Three on a Match*. 1933 *20,000 Years in Sing Sing* / *The Working Man* / *Bureau of Missing Persons* 1934 *Jimmy the Gent* / *Of Human Bondage* 1935 *Bordertown* / *Front Page Woman* / *Dangerous* 1936 *The Petrified Forest* / *Satan Met a Lady* 1937 *Marked Woman* / *Kid Galahad* / *That Certain Woman* / *It's Love I'm After* 1938 *Jezebel* / *The Sisters* 1939 *Dark Victory* / *Juarez* / *The Old Maid* / *The Private Lives of Elizabeth and Essex* 1940 *All This and Heaven Too* / *The Letter* 1941 *The Great Lie* / *The Little Foxes* 1942 *In This Our Life* / *Now, Voyager* 1943 *Watch on the Rhine* / *Old Acquaintance* 1944 *Mr. Skeffington* 1945 *The Corn Is Green* 1946 *A Stolen Life* 1949 *Beyond the Forest* 1950 *All About Eve* 1952 *The Star* 1955 *The Virgin Queen* 1956 *Storm Center* 1961 *Pocketful of Miracles* 1962 *What Ever Happened to Baby Jane?* 1964 *Dead Ringer* / *Where Love Has Gone* 1965 *Hush . . . Hush, Sweet Charlotte* / *The Nanny* 1967 *The Anniversary* 1972 *Madame Sin* (TV) / *The Judge and Jake Wyler* (TV) 1976 *Burnt Offerings* / *The Disappearance of Aimee* (TV) 1978 *Return from Witch Mountain* / *Death on the Nile* 1979 *Strangers: The Story of a Mother and Daughter* (TV) 1980 *White Mama* (TV) / *The Watcher in the Woods* / *Skyward* (TV) 1981 *Family Reunion* (TV) 1982 *A Piano for Mrs. Cimino* (TV) / *Little Gloria . . . Happy at Last* (TV) 1983 *Right of Way* (TV)

THE SEMINAR

Bette Davis held a seminar with the Fellows of the Center for Advanced Film Studies on March 3, 1977.

What do you want from a director?
DAVIS: Oh, I want the world. It's terribly important to have a good director. And a great director in films has a combination of the ability to help you with the performance and the technical knowledge of how to put it together, how to photograph it. There have been very few great directors—Willy Wyler I think is the best of them all. But you couldn't fill two hands with the names of the great directors since I started in 1930.

An actor owes the director a lot. You mustn't just sit around and say, "Yes, yes, yes"—you must have a concept of what you're going to do. You owe that to him as much as he owes that to you. You must trust him and in the long run go by what he says—unless you have an idiot director, of which there are many. Then it's self-preservation to conduct yourself, because in the long run the general public does not know anything about the director or the writer, and you're the one who is going to be blamed.
So you become your own director?
DAVIS: You have to, and that's not ideal at all. I don't think you'll ever be as good in any part as you will with a great director. Even though you may have years and years of experience, you cannot judge yourself. I think often we're very bad judges of ourselves. My mother did a marvelous thing to me once when I was in one of my first plays in New York, *Broken Dishes*. One night I came home and said, "Mother, tonight I was marvelous." Dead silence. She said, "I was there, dear. It was the worst performance you've ever given of that part." You can't allow yourself to enjoy it that much. Then you have lost control.

I have to respect a director enough to give complete trust to him. I haven't had the experience often. A director is like your father, your beau; you often fall in love with the director—not personally, but you have this real feeling. He's like an analyst. Every actor is different to direct; some actors work better if the director is very tough; some are better if he's reasonable. He has to be everything, and you have to feel that he is.

How do you like the director to communicate with you?
DAVIS: Ideally, a director should let the cast rehearse it the way they feel it, maybe many times, and then the director will say, "That's good, that's bad," and put it all together. The director who acts it out for you is ghastly.

We all knew lines, natch. In those days we all knew lines; I must say it's not always that way today. Willy Wyler would just sit there and have his morning coffee and four or five donuts and watch you, saying nothing. Then he'd say, "Do it again." He's learning from you and figuring out what he thinks is good and bad. Then he gets up and says, "Now, I think that cross is not necessary," or this or that. That's ideal.

Willy Wyler and I had only one real professional disagreement, and that was on *The Letter* [1940]. The end of the original play of Mr. Maugham's is the line: "I still love the man I killed." We couldn't end it there because it was a big censorship era and if you murdered anybody you had to die yourself. Of course, it was ridiculous, because to live on with your own guilt is a far worse hell than having somebody happily put you out of your misery. So I never believed that she could look her husband in the eye and say, "I still love the man I killed." I wanted to have it come out without my even knowing I was going to say it. But we ended up doing it Wyler's way. At the dinner the other night [Davis's Life Achievement Award tribute from the AFI] he said he knew I'd still love to run back to Warner Brothers and redo that line the way I wanted to do it. I said, "I would."
In All About Eve *[written and directed by Joseph L. Mankiewicz, 1950], when you said, "Fasten your seatbelts," why did you wait and walk up the stairs before you turned around and did the rest of the line: ". . . it's going to be a stormy night"? Was that a direction from Mankiewicz?*
DAVIS: No, that was my own timing. That's part of your contribution. Seeing her whole back made you know that she was going to say something, that she was collecting herself for her venom. Mankiewicz is a very fine director; he gives the cast their lead rope, and then has excellent ideas.
Would you discuss it first or just jump right in and he'd watch it?
DAVIS: He'd watch it. Or if you had any problem beforehand you'd say, "I don't understand how to play this," which often hap-

pened. I didn't know what in the world to do with Jane [in Robert Aldrich's *What Ever Happened to Baby Jane?*, 1962] until I got into the clothes. We rehearsed one week sitting around the table with the whole cast, and I tried every voice, everything. But when I got into that outfit there wasn't any doubt what to do. Sometimes that happens with a part, you know. It isn't always necessary, but she was a puzzling woman to figure out. And I've played many peculiar women in my career.

Did you always think it was important to know specifically what you wanted before you played a part, or did you prefer not to be that literal?

DAVIS: No, I always was literal—in the beginning *too* literal. Wyler taught me not to be overly specific. I was like the painter who in the beginning draws the perfect lines, and then as he grows in his art, he gradually doesn't do that anymore. But I was overly specific, overly logical. That can be as bad as being too much the other way.

Details like your hairstyle in Little Foxes *[directed by Wyler, 1941] and the candy in* All About Eve—*where did those things come from?*

DAVIS: The candy came from Mr. Mankiewicz. That was the one scene that was really expository. We had to have it for the good of the plot, so I went to him that morning and said, "What can we do with this so it's not just a talky scene?" And he said, "Do you see that candy jar on the piano? The madder you get, the more you want a piece of candy." It was a genius piece of business. Lots of little things, like the hair in *The Little Foxes*, were all from me. Those are things that you should be able to do as an actress and that a director wouldn't think of telling you to do.

When do you bring things like that to a director?

DAVIS: During rehearsal. I think the screen is a fantastic medium for the reality of little things like that, as opposed to the theater, where many such things would be lost. I *adore* the screen. It's more realistic.

Are you speaking of the finished product or the process of work?

DAVIS: The process of acting is basically the same. Some actors miss audiences. I don't happen to. I don't have that feeling about it. The one tragedy of the screen and the one basic thing to learn is how to go out of sequence in the performance. That takes a lot of training in the beginning. I found that very awkward after the theater. But you can learn to do it. Of course, the other bad thing about film is that once it's in the can you can never change it; many times you'll see a scene and say, "Oh, I would have done that better." That is its biggest tragedy. The privilege of the theater is to change it. It's the big advantage the theater has, that and the continuity. I never missed the continuity eventually. I learned to do it. George Arliss said to me on the first film I did with him [*The Man Who Played God,* 1932], "Never do one foot of film without reviewing what is coming before and what is coming after." It's an enormous help to keep that in your mind.

Will you ever go back to the stage?

DAVIS: No. I dislike the stage utterly. I loved it as a kid when I started in it, but it's absolutely exhausting at my age, the eight shows a week. It's not a life at all. You live all day long in a horrible state of fright about the performance that night. And then if it goes well you never want to go to bed because it's the only time you've been happy all day. It's a selfish life. The biggest tragedy is for someone in my position. It's hopeless to have an understudy, because if you're not there they just go and get their money back. The responsibility is like a monkey on your back every minute. Plus, I find acting for the motion pictures more rewarding.

*In the last few days we've seen four of your performances, each a different characterization—*Jezebel *[directed by Wyler, 1938],* The Little Foxes, Of Human Bondage *[directed by John Cromwell, 1934], and* All About Eve. *How do you approach a role?*

DAVIS: Well, listen, without scripts none of us can work. It's the beginning of the work. Somebody asked Claude Rains once what his method was, and he said, "I just learn the lines and pray to God." I am basically in that category. There's no way of explaining what you do. Parts are different. For instance, if you're going to play Queen Elizabeth [Davis played Elizabeth I in *The Private Lives of Elizabeth and Essex,* 1939, and in *The Virgin Queen,* 1955] you read everything you can about her so that you have a basic conception before you start the film. *All About Eve—* well, that was heaven, such gorgeous writing—it was a natural part for me. I was not cast in the beginning; I was a replacement for Claudette Colbert. They said, "You've got to be in San Francisco one week from now." I was finishing another film. I said, "Got to be? I'll be there tomorrow for that part." I always said to Mankiewicz, "You resurrected me from the dead," because that was the most brilliantly written and directed film.

In *Of Human Bondage*, I was very young. I was embarrassed. I was born and brought up in Yankeeland, outside Boston, and I was very inhibited about playing some of the scenes. The director, Mr. Cromwell, said that if I hadn't been born in Boston my career would have been successful ten years earlier. I wasn't experienced enough in life to understand about bondage. I used to go to all my men friends and ask them about it. I never had one man tell me that he had not had this experience. And, of course, when I grew older I found that women have this happen to them, too. None of the established women in this town would play that part. That's the only reason I got it. It was the first bitch heroine that ever was on the screen. But I always believed in character work, so I didn't mind—I went whole hog. Of course, I studied Mr. Maugham's book. That book was a textbook.

When you play such a villainous character, do you ask yourself why she does what she does? Or do you not even think in those terms?

DAVIS: You have to think some about why she does it, of course. But the writing was so clear. Even though I didn't totally understand it, the lines were such that it came out that way. On *Little Foxes* I begged the producer, Samuel Goldwyn, to let Tallulah Bankhead play Regina because Tallulah was magnificent on the stage. He wouldn't let her. He should have, because I had to do that part exactly the way Tallulah did it, because that's the way Miss Hellman wrote it. But I was always sad that Tallulah couldn't record Regina from the theater because she was marvelous.

You don't feel that acting has to be scaled down for the camera?

DAVIS: No, I've always felt that you could be as full emotionally for the camera as for the theater. I've been criticized many times for that by critics; everybody says you shouldn't do as much for the camera, but I don't believe in that.

You've done a lot of daring things on screen, such as shaving your head for the role of Elizabeth.

DAVIS: Every day. That was terrible. From that I understood how men hate to shave. At six in the morning, that noise! And I used to get a black shadow, so they would have to reshave me about five o'clock. Of course, the horror was when the film was over and it started growing out. I tell you, my romantic life was over for quite a while. But that was the only way to do it because she really had no hair.

Yes, but some actresses wouldn't want to do things like that.

DAVIS: Well, that was always my love, to make it look real.

I don't know what you think about Now, Voyager *[directed by Irving Rapper, 1942]—*

DAVIS: If you didn't like it, God help you! It was one of my favorites. I almost didn't get that part. They had cast Irene Dunne, and I went to Hal Wallis [the head of production] and said, "Mr. Wallis, please, because I know those people so well having lived there." Thank God he let me have it.

Did you follow the script with as much fidelity as you did when you filmed a play like Maugham's The Letter?

DAVIS: The script of *Voyager* [by Casey Robinson] was not as good as the book [by Olive Higgins Prouty], so I would go home every night and get that particular part of the book and write it out and bring it in. Because her book was brilliant, and his script was very flowery, overwritten.

How did you make that change in the film from the repressed girl to the sophisticated woman?

DAVIS: It had to be done very subtly. Even though they changed her exterior, she didn't change completely inside for a long time. I understood her so well. She was so totally a Yankee person and had been so mutilated by her mother. As a matter of fact, I sat in a room socially not long after *Voyager*, and Charlotte Vale [the character Davis played] entered with her mother. I tell you, there they were. She had the Buster Brown shoes on and she was about twenty years old, this poor creature. And of course she brought up *Now, Voyager* and how absolutely ridiculous it was, that there wasn't anybody in the world like that. But the reaction to that film was absolutely astronomical, not only from young people with mothers like that but also from many mothers who said they realized what they had been doing wrong.

Have you ever played a part that you loathed?

DAVIS: Oh, many, in the beginning. Terrible things: you know,

parachute jumper, housewife. *The Golden Arrow* [1936] was a dilly. Of course I hated them, but I was in no position to fight them at that time. I was an unknown actress, and they had a right to have me do these ridiculous scripts. *Three on a Match* [1932]—you can't imagine. They were dreadful scripts, *dreadful.*
How did you get through them?
DAVIS: Well, you learned a lot. You learn a lot more, really, in the beginning, from doing things you don't like. Today, because there is no contract system and actors have a complete choice of scripts, I think actors are apt to pick the things they want to do and like to do most, and not progress as much.
Is it true that you and Joan Crawford didn't get along when you made What Ever Happened to Baby Jane?
DAVIS: There's a great misunderstanding that any time two women work together there's automatically going to be a terrific feud. The press did everything in the world to see that Joan and I had a big fight. Well, in the first place, we made *Baby Jane* in three weeks, so we didn't have any time for a feud. If it had been three months, I don't know what would have happened. But in three weeks nothing happened, because we are both professionals. Actually, the men have bigger feuds than the women. It's an old wives' tale that women can't get along, you know. It truthfully is. It's really stupid. Actors basically get along.
How was it working with male stars?
DAVIS: I never worked with Gable or Cooper or most of those big, big male stars. Because, in those days, if you could carry a film yourself you didn't have another star.
Should we mention Errol Flynn?
DAVIS: Errol was one of the most charming people in the world, but if he were sitting right here, he would admit that he did not have an ambition to become a great actor. He loved all the rest of it. In his adventure films he was divine; he was probably the most beautiful-looking thing I've ever seen in my life. But he and I didn't approach work in the same way. He used to think I was ridiculous, because I felt sorry that he didn't love the work more. He was perfectly horrid about me in his book—he said that I scratched his face with my rings—of course, it's all ridiculous; I did no such thing. Those are the little things that helped me become a "monster." But I must say I almost did not do *Elizabeth*

and Essex because of Errol, because he was not up to playing it; that was almost blank verse. Everytime the throne room doors opened I just sat there and closed my eyes and pretended it was Laurence Olivier.

When Dustin Hoffman did Marathon Man *[1976], he had a scene in which he was supposed to have been awake for two or three days, and to play it he stayed up for two or three days. Laurence Olivier, who was in the film, said, "Why doesn't he just* act*? It's so much easier." What do you think of Method acting?*

DAVIS: That is no part of what I believe. No criticism of Hoffman whatsoever, if that's what he has to do. But I think you should be able to just go in and do it. I'm very old-fashioned. That probably works for him. It never would work for me. I don't understand how he could do any lines after being up that long. Makeup can give you that look, you know. That's what makeup is all about. Lots of people think the way he approached it is terrific. But you should be able to indicate it without doing that.

I enjoyed your autobiography.

DAVIS: It was work.

It was a very sad book.

DAVIS: *I'm* sort of sad.

Is that why you called it The Lonely Life?

DAVIS: I think all people in the arts lead lonely lives. Number one, they're totally occupied. They do not have time for friendships. You can't have a great many friends if you don't give a lot of friendship. They have very few outside activities. Certainly in the early years your work is all you do. And you also have a different viewpoint from other people. As I said in the book, you have to travel light. Because we're peculiar people. We're very childlike. I don't think we could become actors if we weren't, because it's pretending, isn't it? That's our approach. And that doesn't help people understand you as a person.

Do you think love interferes with an artist's work?

DAVIS: Love has tempted me from my work, yes. But there was no way. At a very early age I fell in love with my profession. I was well aware that I wasn't going to have the happiest life, but there was nothing I could do about it, I loved it so. The two don't mix very well. It's difficult.

Jeanne Moreau told us that love has never destroyed her passion.
DAVIS: Well, she went very far with her private life. Yes, you can indulge in passion, but to be involved with an actress is an awkward position for a man. It's almost impossible. With all my respect for marriage—I have a deep understanding of the situation of the male—there's nothing you can do. Men think it's not going to bother them when they decide to marry you, but it does. It bothers me, too. So, as my mother said, you cannot have everything in this world. I was lucky that I had three children after the career was made. I spent eighteen marvelous years bringing up three children; that was one of the great parts of my life. So I had the best of two worlds, almost.
In recent years you've done parts in rather macabre pictures—
DAVIS: Yes, three of them in a row. All great parts: *Baby Jane, Hush . . . Hush, Sweet Charlotte* [directed by Robert Aldrich, 1964], and *The Nanny* [directed by Seth Holt, 1965]. But they were extremely difficult films, because you're doing the Hitchcock trick of kidding everybody along until the very end and still having to be believable while you're doing it. Of the three, of course, *Baby Jane* was the most fun.
The latest film I've seen you in is Burnt Offerings *[directed by Dan Curtis, 1976]. Why did you do that?*
DAVIS: Well, you see, at my age, to get any kind of good leading character—it just doesn't come along. I like to work about once a year. It's healthy not to sit at home. This script came along, and at least she was kind of a nice, normal woman who didn't kill anybody, and she didn't go crazy and all that. I have never seen the film and probably never will, because I know instinctively I would hate it. It turned out to be a much bloodier film than I thought it would be. I never saw so much ketchup floating around a set in my life. It wasn't ideal, but there just wasn't anything else for me to do, so I did it.
What are your acting plans for the future?
DAVIS: Well, at this point you don't approach it that way. You just pray to God somebody will send you a script you like. In the old days they wrote scripts for us, they bought things for us. Today they cast films with nobody in mind in the beginning. So you have to be lucky. For instance, we were going to make *David Copperfield* in England, and I would have been Betsy Trotwood,

which would have been great fun, but they can't get the money together for it. It's a wicked business today. So you just keep hoping. When *The Disappearance of Aimee* [the 1976 TV movie, directed by Anthony Harvey, in which Davis was the mother of evangelist Aimee Semple McPherson, played by Faye Dunaway] came along, that was the best writing for me I'd seen in years, so at least I have had that lately [the script was by John McGreevey].
Do you find TV much different from doing feature films?
DAVIS: It's the same. All our films were made with that rapidity in the beginning. *Dark Victory* [1937] was made in four weeks. *Jezebel* was made in six. That's how we were trained. When television started, they weren't going to hire any people like me; they said, "Oh, those actors couldn't possibly make these schedules." But we were trained for it.
Didn't you take out an ad in the trade papers once saying you were looking for work?
DAVIS: Yes, but I *was* working. It wasn't that I really wanted employment. I was making *Baby Jane* at the time. But I was getting completely fed up with the fact that the banks had a list of actors who could make money, and if you weren't on that list no company could hire you. It still exists. This was really a rib on the whole system. I wrote it just like a want ad: "Wanted—employment. Mother of three. Divorced. Thirty years' experience. Reasonably mobile. More affable than rumored."
They say today that there are very few bankable female stars.
DAVIS: Well, there aren't any scripts for females. It's not the female time. It will change. We had it for twenty years. One actor said then, "The only thing the leading man in a film has to be sure of is that his haircut in the back is in perfect shape." Yes, there were women's pictures for all those years, and it's now been men's films for many years. But it changes with the world. The problems of the world have become men's problems, the crime and all the other ghastly things that are going on today involve men much more than women. I think if there is talent it will always work itself out. But it is a bad period for women in films, there's no question.
If you were starting again today, would you want to be an actress?
DAVIS: If I knew what I know now about the business, having been in it so long, I'd give it much more thought than I did then.

It's very rough today. The tragedy is that because so few films are being made, television series are definitely it. And if you get into a successful series you play that one part for maybe three years. Under the contract system, month after month after month we were allowed to make films. And we learned something from even the dreadful ones, so we had a great chance to improve ourselves. Working all the time is the only way. There are such spaces today between films, even for the women who are getting along well. The public makes stars, not the studios. They either take you unto themselves or they don't. And that has a lot to do with how often you are seen.

Do you think that the little foxes have taken over the industry?

DAVIS: There was always an enormous difference between the artistic side of the industry and the money side, between the men who ran the studios and those of us on the stages. Neither of us understood the other at all. Artistically, it was extraordinarily difficult, always. I don't think it's terribly different today. I think with some of the independent productions there are more intelligent people on the producing end today—Alan Pakula and people like that. But the money situation is worse today than it was then. And the schedules—it's no fun anymore: "Just get it done." They always were wanting us to get it done on time, but there wasn't that terrible pressure there is today.

What sort of advice or perhaps encouragement do you have for actors and actresses who dissipate their energy working in nine-to-five office jobs just to pay the rent and don't have the energy to pursue their art?

DAVIS: Oh, what to say? What to say? I think acting is something that you absolutely have to do—there's no way you can stop yourself—it means that much. If you don't feel that dedication, it's a terrible profession. And nowadays it's very spotty earning money because there is no contract system. We were paid every week, no matter how little we worked, so we could support ourselves in the beginning without doing other jobs. It's a purely personal approach, and it takes a lot of guts.

I guess that's a backhanded encouragement. Thank you.

DAVIS: Yes. But if you love it, oh, your rewards. It takes a lot of years. I'll end now, as I did the other night, with my favorite line I've ever had to say. It came out of *Cabin in the Cotton* [1932]: "Ah'd love to kiss ya, but ah jest washed mah hair."

John A. Alonzo

Critics have observed that the best thing about most Hollywood films of the 1970s was their cinematography, and John A. Alonzo is among the best of the new breed of cameramen. The outspoken and ambitious Alonzo has also been successfully pursuing a parallel career as a director.

Some of his most notable photography has been on such period films as *Sounder, Lady Sings the Blues, Chinatown, The Fortune,* and *Farewell, My Lovely,* in which he has contributed a distinctive sepia sheen to the visuals. His other major credits include the cult classic *Harold and Maude, The Bad News Bears,* and *Norma Rae.*

Alonzo began his Hollywood career as an actor, and that experience helped him make the transition to directing on the 1978 feature *FM.* Since then he has directed as well as photographed four TV movies—*Champions: A Love Story, Portrait of a Stripper, Belle Starr,* and *Blinded by the Light.*

The first Mexican-American cameraman in the Hollywood union, Alonzo was born in Dallas in 1934 and spent the first ten years of his life in Nuevo Laredo, Mexico. His father was a migratory farmworker and his mother was a cook. Although Alonzo

117

had difficulty becoming a cinematographer, he attributes his slow start to industry cronyism rather than prejudice.

As a young man in Dallas he swept floors at a legitimate theater and at WFAA-TV before becoming a TV cameraman and director while still in his teens. Moving to Hollywood in 1956, he had his own puppet show on KHJ-TV and began acting in TV series and such films as *The Magnificent Seven* and *Invitation to a Gunfighter*.

After he photographed two short films, *The Rainbow in the Sand* and *The Legend of Jimmy Blue Eyes* (the latter receiving an Oscar nomination), David Wolper Productions hired him as a documentary cameraman. He spent several years shooting TV documentaries, including Jacques Cousteau and *National Geographic* specials and two acclaimed films directed by William Friedkin, *Mayhem on a Sunday Afternoon* and *The Thin Blue Line*.

Cinematographer James Wong Howe and director John Frankenheimer, after hiring Alonzo for three days' work as an operator on *Seconds* (1966), helped him obtain his union card. Alonzo's first feature as director of photography was Roger Corman's *Bloody Mama* in 1970.

His career acquired momentum after Howe recommended him to director Martin Ritt for *Sounder*, the outstanding 1972 film about black sharecroppers in the South of the 1930s. Alonzo and Ritt have continued their fruitful partnership on six other films, including *Norma Rae* and their most recent work, *Cross Creek*.

Remembering his own difficulties in entering the business, Alonzo, along with a group of other newly established cameramen, has been active in modernizing union work rules and eligibility requirements for aspiring talent.

FILMOGRAPHY (feature-length)

1970 *Bloody Mama*   1971 *Vanishing Point* / *Harold and Maude* / *Revenge* (TV)   1972 *Get to Know Your Rabbit* / *Sounder* / *Lady Sings the Blues* / *Pete 'n' Tillie*   1973 *The Naked Ape* / *Hit!* / *Wattstax*   1974 *Conrack* / *Chinatown*

1975 *The Fortune* / *Once Is Not Enough* / *Farewell, My Lovely*
1976 *I Will, I Will . . . for Now* / *The Bad News Bears* / *Look
What's Happened to Rosemary's Baby* (TV) 1977 *Black Sun-
day* / *Close Encounters of the Third Kind* (additional photogra-
phy) 1978 *Casey's Shadow* / *FM* (director only) / *The Cheap
Detective* 1979 *Champions: A Love Story* (TV; also director) /
Norma Rae / *Portrait of a Stripper* (TV; also director) 1980
Tom Horn / *Belle Starr* (TV; also director) / *Blinded by the
Light* (TV; also director) 1981 *Back Roads* / *Zorro, the Gay
Blade* 1982 *The Kid from Nowhere* (TV) 1983 *Blue Thun-
der* / *Cross Creek*

THE SEMINAR

John A. Alonzo held seminars with Fellows of the Center for Advanced Film Studies in conjunction with the American Society of Cinematographers on December 4, 1974, and for the Center for Advanced Film Studies alone on November 5, 1975.

What do you think is the ideal relationship between a cinematographer and a director?
ALONZO: I prefer a director who is totally prepared, who has shot the film in his dreams as many times as I have. It's a compliment when a director says, "I don't know what I want to do—tell me where you want to put the camera," but it's also dangerous. Suppose it doesn't turn out right; you've taken on a big responsibility. I like the responsibility, but I like to make sure that the director and I share it. I want to have the security that when he makes a decision, it's a good decision.

I also like a director to have as much knowledge as possible about my job, because it cuts through an awful lot of red tape and explanation, and it helps him a great deal. Some of you may think, "Why does a director want to know what a lens does?" but that's important for all of us. Film is a collaborative art form, but it doesn't function unless we all know what the others do. I've made it a point to learn a lot about directing and writing. I don't have any hang-ups about wanting to direct, but I do like to stick my nose into it if I feel it's affecting the visual aspect of the picture. I like to have a director give me the freedom of giving him different ways of composing and lighting. I like to have the confidence that he's relying on my ability.

Do you discuss the look of a picture extensively with the director before you begin shooting?
ALONZO: I nearly go to bed with him. I read a piece of material and I get my own interpretation of it. Then I talk to the director and get his idea of how he wants it interpreted on film, what mood the light will establish, whether or not to put light on people, and so forth. I feed on what he's saying. Then I rely on my own ability to keep a continuity in the lighting when I shoot out of sequence. That is very much like what a director does

when he's directing actors and keeps in mind where the little pieces go in the puzzle.

Martin Ritt [the director for whom Alonzo shot *Sounder* in 1972 and *Conrack* in 1974] likes to have not only the cameraman but the production designer and editor around from the beginning of preparation. We may spend hours drinking coffee and talking, but out of those hours may come a couple of key phrases that allow me to get into the director's head and vice versa.

Sounder is my love affair. The key to the look of the picture for me was the artist Andrew Wyeth. James Wong Howe was going to shoot *Sounder*, but he was ill. Jimmy had helped me get into the union in 1966, and he called me up to talk about *Sounder*; it was very nice of him. He said, "Get a good hook on it. Look at some pictures and books and give Marty some choices, because he likes to work that way." I told Marty about this conversation, and he said, "Yes, think of the word 'lyrical.'" I had studied art in Mexico; I already knew about Wyeth, but I went out and found some interesting compositions of his and some gorgeous portraits he did of black people.

I approached Marty with what I found. They had built a little set for the house, and I said, "Get really old wood for the inside, with a lot of grain and dark brown colors." He was worried about what we would get on film when we photographed a black person against a dark background, but I said I could handle it, and Wyeth was the key. Marty left me totally alone on that picture. He would rehearse his actors, and he'd say, "We'll put the camera right here." I would pick the lens, and we'd shoot.

I've noticed your fondness for muted colors, the predominance of browns and blacks, not only in Sounder *but also in* Harold and Maude *[directed by Hal Ashby, 1972] and* Chinatown *[directed by Roman Polanski, 1974]. How much of that is the production designer's contribution and how much is your own approach to color?*

ALONZO: It's personal taste. I'm partial to brown; I love brown. And I think we really see that way. Everything isn't as bright as Eastman Color makes it out to be. If you keep the color subdued when you're shooting a picture, you can use it as a painter does: when you want to shock people, you throw color at them. You paint it. In *Farewell, My Lovely* [directed by Dick Richards, 1975] I used as much color as I could in certain places because I felt it added to the bizarreness of the situation.

I always work closely with the production designer and the director on the overall look of the film. On *Harold and Maude*, Hal Ashby and I thought we would make all of Harold's [Bud Cort's] sequences cold and crisp-looking, and all of Maude's [Ruth Gordon's] warm and toasty. But there are things in *Harold and Maude* I wish I could do over again, because I was still very new at what I was doing. I used too much diffusion, too many fog filters [devices to make the image soft and hazy]. I used them except in sequences where I pulled the filters off to accentuate the colors. When they're sitting out by the dumps among the sea-gulls on San Francisco Bay, I took the fog off because God did a very nice job of lighting there.

I didn't start *Chinatown* [Alonzo replaced the original cam-eraman, Stanley Cortez, early in the shooting]. The production designer, Richard Sylbert, had already done the sets, and Anthea Sylbert had done the costumes. I let Dick spray lacquer over every piece of wood on the sets; I was trying for very low-key [dark] lighting, and I felt the shiny wood at least would give me some perspective lighting in places it would be too dark to illuminate. The selection of the color was made after the film was finished [that is, in making the prints]. I helped it along by putting Chinese tracing paper on the sets, which has a soft, brownish texture. And outside the windows of the sets we used black-and-white backdrops, not color, to give a monochromatic look. When we made the release prints at Technicolor, we worked reel after reel for this sepia tone, and we finally came up with the color I thought was right.

We showed it to Robert Evans [the producer], Robert Towne [the writer], and Jack Nicholson [the star] at Evans's house, because he's got the best projection system in town. Afterward, Bob Evans asked for opinions, and Jack said, "I don't like the color." I like Jack for his honesty, but he wasn't articulate enough for me. He said, "I liked it the way it was in the dailies. Why can't we have it like that?" I said, "What was so good about the dailies?" He said, "Well, I don't know. They were whitish-brown."

Bob Evans said, "Maybe what Jack means is that it's a little too yellow." Bob Towne was also on Jack's side.

This was on a Thursday night, and the following Monday they had to have twelve prints in New York, Chicago, and Los Angeles. I got together with Bob Van Andle and Mike Crane from Technicolor, and we tried another print. We subtracted yellow from it, and we ended up with a browner look. I ended up liking it very much, but that was pure luck. The next time I saw Jack was at the Directors Guild screening; he said, "That was it. It's perfect."

I try to keep an open mind. You can't become prejudiced against any way of doing things, because then you're negating your ability to expand.

Do you prefer now to adjust the color and the exposure of the film in post-production rather than flashing the negative [exposing it to light] before shooting or using filters while you're shooting?

ALONZO: I never do anything to the negative in the camera if I can help it, because I may change my mind later. I feel that I should give the negative a good middle exposure and then screw around with it later, in the printing, rather than overexposing or underexposing too much.

All cameramen should be knowledgeable about the chemistry, the mathematics, the mechanics of cinematography. It should be almost second nature. That leaves you freer to get more esthetically involved and become keener in what you see. You must also have an understanding of natural light. What is natural light? Light that you can't control, what God does for you outdoors. And you must know how to use artificial light to reproduce natural lighting. With those things thoroughly ensconced in your brain, you can now deal with a director on a social level, a political level, and an esthetic level, and your brain is freer to work. You can work more like an artist.

What principles are involved in making a set look like a real place?

ALONZO: How do you do reality? You study the light sources. Don't alter them; intensify them. That doesn't mean you can't double-cross the rules. If you don't feel like using the source light, play with it, do something else. But keep it consistent. The biggest mistake cameramen make is not to have a visual continuity. They'll shoot a sequence according to what they feel at the time. But because we're getting more chances now to work with the director in preparing the film, we can start with a visual continuity. Even if we shoot the last shot of the film first, we can say, "That's the style, so every shot has to have that style." When a director starts to get away from that style, I'll remind him. If he can convince me that he'd rather do it another way, I start changing my game plan. Some cameramen become selfish and don't want to change their plans. But because I'm an ex-actor and I've directed my dinky little things [Alonzo later directed his first feature, *FM*, in 1978], I feel for a director; their problems are horrendous. They've got so much to worry about that the last thing they want is a confrontation with their right arm, the cameraman.

How much do you rely on a light meter in judging the exposure of a shot?

ALONZO: When I didn't know anything about exposure I owned only one light meter, and now that I don't need a meter I have every one in the book. Don't become dependent on the light meter. Become dependent on your eye and on what you think it should look like. I use my own eye a great deal, unless there's a specific effect to go for. I do use a meter sometimes when an actor or actress is going through a tremendous amount of light changes; I'll follow the face through the scene to see how it does. But the best experience you can have is just to shoot so much film that you know what it does, and use the meter only as a guide.

Could you talk about the problems involved in location shooting as opposed to studio shooting, and what you look for when you scout locations?

ALONZO: It depends on the project. If it's a period film, when you're scouting locations you try to keep all the things that are not of the period out of the picture. If it's a present-day film, my only concerns are where the lighting sources are on the location—where the sun is coming from, where the electrical power is so you don't have to spend a lot of money on generators—and what kind of apparatus I might need for the camera, such as a crane or a car mount. I scout the locations so that if a location has a complementary set on a stage—if we have to cut from the exterior of the real one into the interior of the phony one—I control the lighting on location so that I can match the stage lighting to it as closely as possible.

You started in documentaries. How is that different for a cameraman from shooting features?

ALONZO: I love documentaries. One of these days I'll say, "Hey, fellows, see you later," and go back to doing that. The best time my wife and I had was when we were in Australia for three months shooting a documentary. We also spent seven or eight weeks in Yellowstone National Park shooting a documentary on grizzly bears, and another time we went to Alaska and Africa filming wolves. The nice thing about it is that you have to prepare in your head and visualize. There was no money to scout locations ahead of time. I think it's the best training ground a filmmaker can have: you have to figure out all the variables, and since you can't take all the equipment with you, you're stuck with what you have and you have to do things with it.

Do you use a zoom lens very much and if not, why?

ALONZO: A zoom lens is a wonderful lens that has been overused. I used to go bananas with it in documentaries, but [producer David L.] Wolper used to make the cameramen assemble their own footage and log it [record information about each shot in a log book for reference during editing], and I finally got sick of watching myself zoom, zoom, zoom. I made up my mind that there are specific uses for the zoom lens, and it has to be in relationship with what the writer and the director intend. If I have to use a zoom because it's physically impossible to move the camera that close, I try to dolly and zoom at the same time [to disguise the fact that he is zooming], and I select a focal length that doesn't destroy the perspective of the set or of the object. In *Harold and Maude* we used zoom lenses judiciously, I thought, because a bizarre style was called for by the story.

What kind of lighting do you suggest in documentaries so as not to make the subject uncomfortable or distract him?

ALONZO: That's the biggest problem. It destroys a person who has to be subjected to very hot lighting. I would try to use available light as much as possible. If I were shooting you, the only thing I might do would be to put up a white card and bounce the light off it into your eyes. You don't want to put the light right over the lens, because a person who is not an actor would be distracted. I would throw the lights way the hell out of the way; I would move myself as far away from the subject as possible and let the interviewer be the only person in close proximity. Never get on top of a person you're photographing, especially a non-pro. Even when you're shooting a feature it's a good thing to remember. In *Chinatown* we purposely shot with 40-millimeter [wide-angle] lenses on top of Faye Dunaway, because it's intimidating, and it adds to the drama. Roman kept her nervous and keyed up all the time, even off-stage. We were a little concerned about it, but there was method in his madness.

In feature cinematography you have an advantage over documentary in having an art director and a director who can cooperate with you. You can say to Jack Nicholson, "If Polanski says it's OK, would you mind pausing for a moment in front of that light bulb?" You have that kind of control, and I do try to get the best composition possible. But I can't allow myself to go too far in that direction. I can't shoot a movie just to assuage my own ego; it has to be something that complements what the writer had in mind, what the director wants done, and what the actors contribute.

A lot of cameramen and directors have been saying they wish Technicolor had not dropped the imbibition process in its Hollywood laboratory [a system of color processing used there until 1974 that provided richer and more durable hues; Chinatown *was one of the last Hollywood films made in the process]. Isn't there any way cameramen could make them go back to it?*

ALONZO: They gave it up because of the expense. It's very disheartening. Studios no longer buy five or six hundred prints at a time, and it's a very expensive process. The new film stock, 5247, was brought in because now the labs are able to process twice as much material. Most of the technical changes in our industry are economic. Cameras are not designed from an esthetic point of view but according to what is economically feasible. They design a faster lens so that we don't have to use as much light. They invent a longer zoom so that we don't have to move the camera. They design a hand-held camera so that we don't have to use a tripod. Those are the premises of designing a lot of the equipment. I'm a big fan of Panavision [a firm that makes cameras and lenses] because they design equipment and don't really care if it's going to cost a fortune to rent. They're designing it because they think they can provide a better piece of equipment to give you a broader base to operate on artistically. And Cinema Research [a firm that does visual effects and opticals, such as dissolves] designed a machine to correct an esthetic problem with grainy dissolves; they didn't do it to make more money through opticals, because they won't—they'll make the same. Those guys had their heads on right. Those are a couple of instances in which someone is helping filmmakers by giving us some better tools, some better paintbrushes.

How do you resolve the problem of trying to achieve the best possible lighting of a scene while adapting to the director's blocking of the actors?

ALONZO: Ever since I shot *Sounder*, I've tried to light in such a way that there are no rules for the actors and they don't have to stop in a certain spot. But on *Once Is Not Enough* [directed by Guy Green, 1975] and *Farewell, My Lovely*, we went for the old style of lighting: control. We told the actors, "You've got to hit these marks" [move according to precise floor markings]. But most of the time I try not to. There have been moments in pictures I have shot, such as *Vanishing Point* [directed by Richard Sarafian, 1971], when the actor was far more important than whether or not I composed perfectly. In *Lady Sings the Blues* [directed by Sidney Furie, 1972], there were some scenes in which I couldn't get absolutely controlled composition. Diana Ross had never done a picture before, so she wasn't used to the idea of hitting marks for lights, and Sidney Furie was doing a lot of improvisational material. But most of the time I am led by my own beliefs in what I think is good composition and what I think is esthetically correct.

What are the differences between shooting a movie for television and shooting a feature?

ALONZO: I shot four TV movies as an exercise to see how fast my crew and I could operate. We were going for esthetics at the same time that we were going for page count, fifteen pages per day [on a major feature film, the average is usually between two to four pages per day]. My guys could do that with no problem. I did it because I was getting in a box—people were saying, "Alonzo can't shoot a TV movie; he's a feature cameraman." After I did TV movies they said, "He doesn't shoot features."

What corners do you cut to speed up your work?

ALONZO: We have to work with our director on this, but I concentrate on setting up a lighting style with no change of lighting from master to close-up. In television movies you shoot more close-ups than you do in features. They would never allow some of the long shots you saw in *Harold and Maude*; some clown will say, "It doesn't have enough presence" or something. And on TV movies you can say to the director, "If you want efficiency, we shoot the scene right by the window; we don't have her walk from here to over there." If he says no, OK, but most of the time the TV director is in the same bind you're in, so he wants the most efficient ideas he can get. Especially since the advent of television, most cameramen have learned to work fast whether they like it or not.

Do you generally work from pre-production sketches in planning the shots in a film?

ALONZO: I like working that way. A lot of cameramen tell me that in the past the art director was sort of a bastard child, and they didn't really want to work with him. Nowadays we find it's an advantage. You may never shoot the storyboard exactly, but it gives you a guideline. It depends on the director. I have a hundred and four pages of pictures for my next film, *Black Sunday*, because John Frankenheimer [the director] likes storyboards. On *Sounder* and *Conrack* we had sketches by the art director, Walter Herndon. We didn't have storyboards on *Chinatown*, but Roman and I did a lot of drawing on the floor with chalk, and we'd get into violent arguments about composition.

What was the visual concept you and Polanski had for Chinatown?

ALONZO: What Roman wanted was to shoot the whole picture with a given lens. If you noticed, the point of view of the picture was that of someone looking over Jack Nicholson's shoulder. That was the style Roman wanted. In anamorphic [a wide-screen format in which the image is squeezed onto the negative and unsqueezed when projected], the closest lens to the human eye is a 40-millimeter lens. There is a slight distortion, but the perspective is correct, and it doesn't bend lines. I tried to get Roman to let me compose in such a way that all the vertical lines in a set were parallel to the frame lines, so that it wouldn't have a subconscious distracting effect on the audience. When you're shooting human beings in conversation it's a good rule of thumb: don't distract the audience. My favorite artists are people like Orozco, Tamayo, and Siqueiros, who are very symmetrical in their design and love the mural kind of composition. I like the anamorphic format for that reason.

Roman would take a long time moving around with his viewfinder, finding where we should put the camera. He is very knowledgeable about cinematography, and he has a very good sense of the camera's relationship with people. In *Chinatown* points of view are very important. When Faye Dunaway comes down the stairs and gives Jack the address where her daughter is being held prisoner and Jack realizes it's Chinatown, the point of view was the place below the stairs from which Roman was watching the rehearsal. It didn't have to be Jack's point of view or Faye's point of view; Roman didn't want to look down at Jack at that moment. We both came to the conclusion that it was best to let the audience look at Jack over here and Faye over there, rather than simply taking their points of view.

Who decided on the camera movements?

ALONZO: That was all Roman's, the entire concept. I can't say enough about this man. The weekend before I took over the picture, I saw *Repulsion* and *Cul-de-Sac* [films Polanski made in England in 1964 and 1966], and we talked film the entire Saturday and Sunday, to get into each other's heads. He knows exactly where all the pieces fit. All of the camera movements were precisely worked out. I would look at a shot, I would operate it once in rehearsal, my operator would do it with me watching the camera, and then Roman would look through the viewfinder to make sure the camera ended up where he wanted it. It's precision work.

Were the night scenes of Nicholson at the reservoir shot on location or on a sound stage? The color of the sky seemed unusually vivid.

ALONZO: That's the magic hour [the hour when the sun sets, dubbed the "magic hour" by cameramen because of its unpredictable and often "magical" light]. Roman let me start rehearsing there about two in the afternoon with the camera crew, and then he asked Jack to rehearse it with us, so we got all the mechanics out of the way. Around five-thirty or six P.M., when the light was beginning to get right, we shot that sequence three times in continuity, so that the sky got darker and darker throughout the sequence. A cameraman can't get that kind of opportunity unless he has the cooperation of the director.

Jerry Goldsmith

One of the busiest and most honored contemporary Hollywood composers, Jerry Goldsmith has been described by critics as a composer who writes serious music for films. About half of his more than ninety film scores have been issued on albums, and some have been played in concert halls.

Valued by producers and directors for his keen dramatic sense as well as his musical ability, Goldsmith won an Academy Award for *The Omen* and has been nominated nine other times. He has also won four Emmys, for *The Red Pony, QB VII, Babe,* and *Masada,* and has been nominated for seven Grammy Awards.

Among his notable film scores are *Lonely Are the Brave, Freud, Lilies of the Field, Seven Days in May, A Patch of Blue, The Blue Max, The Sand Pebbles, Planet of the Apes, The Ballad of Cable Hogue, Patton, The Wild Rovers, Chinatown, Islands in the Stream, Star Trek,* and *Poltergeist.*

Born in Los Angeles in 1930, Goldsmith studied piano with Jakob Gimpel, composition with Mario Castelnuevo-Tedesco, and film composing with Miklos Rosza at the University of Southern California. He began scoring radio dramas while a student at Los Angeles City College, and was hired as a composer by CBS Radio while still in his early twenties, scoring such series as *Romance* and *Suspense*.

He worked extensively in series television, beginning with the live drama program *Climax* in 1955. His other series work has included *The Hallmark Hall of Fame, Playhouse 90, Studio One, The Twilight Zone, General Electric Theater, Gunsmoke, Doctor Kildare, Thriller, The Man from UNCLE,* and *The Waltons*.

His first important film score was for *Lonely Are the Brave* in 1962. By the mid-1960s, with his scores for such films as *Lilies of the Field, A Patch of Blue,* and *The Sand Pebbles,* he had reached the front rank of Hollywood composers.

Goldsmith's range is extraordinary: he has written equally memorable scores for Westerns, suspense dramas, love stories, science-fiction, horror films, and historical epics. He has escaped typecasting partially because of his technical flexibility; according to the demands of the film, he has used everything from old-fashioned symphonic orchestration to small jazz combos, electronic scoring, and other avant-garde techniques.

In recent years he has become increasingly active in concert conducting and composing. He made his debut on the concert podium in 1969 with the Southern California Chamber Symphony, conducting his own cantata, *Christus Apollo,* with a text by Ray Bradbury. Since then he has conducted the Unione Musiche di Roma and the Kurt Granke Orchestra in Munich, and was a guest conductor with the Royal Philharmonic Orchestra in London. He has also written music for two ballets, *Othello* and *A Patch of Blue,* the latter adapted from his film score.

SELECTED FILMOGRAPHY

1957 *Black Patch*   1959 *City of Fear*   1960 *Studs Lonigan* 1962 *Lonely Are the Brave | Freud*   1963 *The Stripper | Lilies of the Field*   1964 *Seven Days in May*   1965 *In Harm's Way | A Patch of Blue | Our Man Flint*   1966 *The Blue Max | Seconds | The Sand Pebbles*   1968 *Planet of the Apes | The Detective*   1969 *The Illustrated Man | Justine*   1970 *The Ballad of Cable Hogue | Patton | Tora, Tora, Tora | Rio Lobo*   1971 *The Mephisto Waltz | The Wild Rovers*   1972 *The Other*

1973 *Papillon* / *The Red Pony* (TV)   1974 *Chinatown*   1975
QB VII (TV)   1976 *The Omen* / *Logan's Run* / *The Wind
and the Lion* / *Babe* (TV)   1977 *MacArthur* / *Stakeout on
Cherry Street* (TV) / *Islands in the Stream*   1978 *Coma* / *Magic*
1979 *Alien* / *The Boys from Brazil* / *Star Trek*   1981 *Outland* /
Raggedy Man / *Masada* (TV)   1982 *Inchon* / *Poltergeist* / *First
Blood*   1983 *Psycho II* / *The Twilight Zone*

THE SEMINAR

Jerry Goldsmith held seminars with the Fellows of the Center for Advanced Film Studies on April 30, 1975; May 18, 1977; and July 13, 1978.

What are the things music cannot do for a film?
GOLDSMITH: It cannot do a lot of things. First of all, it cannot save a film. Good films have saved bad music, but even a great score never saved a bad film. And many times the director has felt that by some subtle nuance in the music it would be possible to put across an intellectual point. That really is not possible. I don't know what else music can't do. I'd rather work with what music *can* do.

Each film is different. Each film has a certain problem. Music must somehow emphasize and comment on those elements that are not apparent visually or emotionally on the screen. In *Chinatown* [directed by Roman Polanski, 1974], for example, without music one never felt the love relationship between Faye Dunaway and Jack Nicholson. She dies at the end, and if you don't care about them, the picture's a disaster. I felt I solved that problem as well as it could be done. But too many directors say, "Oh, my God, I've made a bad cut here. Put five seconds of music there." I'm not a patcher-upper.

There was no deficiency in *Patton* [directed by Franklin Schaffner, 1970; starring George C. Scott], but it was a challenge to keep the audience aware of the complexity of Patton's personality. We were dealing with three different facets of Patton's imagination. He was a warrior, a man who believed in reincarnation, and a man with stern religious beliefs. Frank and I felt it was important for the music to help delineate which facet of his personality was predominant in the various scenes. Like any other art form, music has a structure, and if one wants to make a statement that will evoke emotions and recall a certain idea, it has to be planted at the beginning and developed. At the beginning of the picture I set up the reincarnation theme with the trumpet fanfare, the very first notes of music you hear. When he relived the battle of Carthagenia in his mind you heard these trumpets again, heralding this facet of his personality. The second and most obvious piece of music was the military march, and when he was commanding, this was the predominant theme—the warrior theme. The third was a chorale, which was used in counterpoint to underline his religious character, his discipline, and his determination. When he was the whole man, commanding his troops in victory, the idea was to combine all these musical elements, because he was all of these facets together.

I don't think it's something you notice consciously. But music is not supposed to make you say, "Hey, look what they're telling us"; you might as well use subtitles. I think *Patton* was the most extreme and difficult assignment I have had in terms of treating a complex character musically, so that the music has a life of its own and still functions dramatically.

You've worked with a lot of directors, from Sam Peckinpah to Richard Fleischer and Alan Pakula. Could you talk about how you work with a director on approaching the score for a film?

GOLDSMITH: It depends on the director. The only director who brought me in before the shooting was Otto Preminger [on *In Harm's Way*, 1965], and that was a waste of time. A composer doesn't get anything out of sitting on a sound stage. I prefer not to become involved until I actually see the picture. I prefer not to read the script, because we are dealing in a visual medium; I get the product at its next-to-final state.

My reactions on first seeing the film are terribly important. A lot of people are shocked when I say I don't want to read the script, but I explain that I must react to a motion picture as an audience would. I try my damnedest to sit down as a guy who has bought his ticket and his popcorn and says, "I want to be entertained." The important thing is the story. I don't want to know how it's going to end. If I do, my reaction can't be honest. I want to be on the edge of my seat. Many times I'm the first person to see the film. I see it before the head of the studio does. So they're very interested in my reaction as an audience.

I have a problem in doing that, because from the first time I see a film, I start thinking in terms of what I am going to do musically. It's the fear of the blank page; to overcome it, I must go back and see the picture a few more times, because I'm missing a lot of values. Some pictures I can see the first time and come away with a very clear idea of what I'm going to do. Others I can see over and over again and not have the foggiest idea.

After seeing the picture, I will go away and analyze my feelings. Too many directors want to discuss the music on an intellectual basis. Music is maybe the only art that you cannot intellectualize, and 99 percent of directors have little, if any, formal musical training, so I try to eliminate this kind of discussion. If I start talking in terms of instruments or musical forms, the filmmaker is not going to know what the hell I'm talking about nine-tenths of the time, so I'm going to end up talking about dramatic terms, which is what I should be talking about. It's only the dramatics that I'm interested in.

Certain directors, such as Frank Schaffner, *are* terribly musical, having not just a love of music but, more important, a great knowledge of what music and drama can do in combination. I've had a relationship with Frank that goes back seventeen years. Each time we do a project together, we get to know each other more and more, so that we have a freer exchange of ideas.

For instance, on *Papillon* [1973], when Schaffner said, "I feel a melody reminiscent of Montmartre," that was fine. That's easy to identify with. This was after a lot of preliminary discussion. It's important for the director to say to the composer first, "Look, this is the picture I made. Now, what do you think of it? Do you like the picture? What do you see in it? Is there anything you don't understand? How does this scene strike you?" The scenes he asks about usually will be the ones he has a doubt about. And he should say to the composer, "What do you feel about it? How do you want to approach this musically?"

I let the director know my reactions to the film, and where I think music could be a help. I don't talk about what kind of music I'm going to write, because I don't know. I have to wait until I sit down and totally occupy myself with musical concepts. You can get into a trap if you try to impress the director with a lot of verbalization. If you say you're going to have six saxophones and then you don't use them, the director says, "You said you were going to use six saxophones," and I have to say, "Well, I made a mistake. I changed my mind."

One of the problems I face all the time comes when someone

has made a film and he knows what's on the screen is not what he intended. The last resort—after he has cut, recut, and done everything he can—is the music. But if it's not there on the screen, I can't do it. If the director feels insecure with a scene or feels he has not achieved his intention, then he has to examine it honestly, dump his insecurities, and say, "Look, I'm asking for the impossible. I didn't get what I wanted. Is there a creative way that we might put a different slant on this scene, maybe even add some humor to it, something that will work dramatically within the context of the whole film?"

If a director *tells* me what to do musically, that inhibits me terribly. A good director knows the people he's working with and has the faith in those people to let them make their contribution. No intelligent director is going to demand that you do something against your will. If I'm asked to do something that I don't feel, I can manufacture it, because I have experience and technique, but it isn't going to be good. It isn't going to be me.

Is it advisable to have directors exposed to any kind of musical training so they can communicate better with the composer?

GOLDSMITH: A little knowledge is dangerous. The saying in Hollywood is that everyone knows his own job and music too. There's one marvelous director who plays the piano very well, but I must say I totally disagree with his idea of what music should be in a film. People who make films should understand what music can do for a film, the way they understand the camera, the use of a prop, what the art director does. I don't think a good director could come to the cameraman with some of the stupid requests that I get. Perhaps directors feel that if they talk to me in musical terms it's going to make our communication better. It won't. That isn't what I'm looking for. I am a dramatist at this point. I just happen to express my dramatic feelings in a more abstract form.

The director has to understand what he's dealing with. Music is a potent force—the most powerful of all arts. I can take any scene and twist it any way I want it to go. Music can do that. The director has to stop and say honestly to himself, "What is it that I want from the music, and can music give that to me? If this scene is not working, can music make it work?" Then we're starting a dialogue. When I do a Schaffner film we talk practically every day. There is an emotional dialogue between us. There is always some pertinent comment, maybe two lines or one word. Too often the director will disappear for six weeks, and that's tough, because I may want to re-examine a particular scene with him if I have a problem. The more you communicate, the happier both people are going to be with the end result.

Keep it in dramatic and emotional terms. Minimize the intellectual. Talk about gut-level reactions, what both of you feel. Talk to the director about the emotions he was feeling when he made the film, and about how his emotions changed. Many times I have found that a filmmaker has a totally different concept of his film after he has finished it. On two films which shall be nameless, when the directors heard the music they said, "I didn't realize we had a love story there." It amazes me that a person could spend two years on a project and not understand what he's got, but sometimes it's understandable because they are too close to this project; they've been living with it night and day for two years.

One director I admire will never see the picture on the screen until he's finished making his cut. Then he will screen it, go back to his cutting room, and start again. Each time he sees it on the screen, he gets a whole new perspective. But the guy who cuts a reel and runs to the projection room with it soon loses his objectivity.

Some directors who have spoken with us have said that when they're cutting a film they put in a temporary score from records. How do you feel about that?

GOLDSMITH: Sometimes it's my own music they've tracked it with, which is both flattering and annoying. I wish they wouldn't do it. When they put this music in, and they hear it over and over, they start to like it, no matter how ill-fitting it is. It's a curse for me because I may think I should go that way. Whenever that's happened, I've gotten myself into a trap. So I insist that there be no temporary music. If they want to cut it to music, fine; I can write some music they can record temporarily on the piano so they have the rhythm. That should be the way to do it, but that doesn't happen.

One of the problems I have discovered is that directors become insecure when they're editing film and there's no music. If you like the effect of a truck passing and you feel that is an important dramatic point, just use that. Why have music? There are marvelous moments without music. I'm not writing a concert. Sometimes the less music there is, the more emphasis it has. *Patton* was almost three hours long, and there were only about thirty-two minutes of music in the picture. But the music had a great impact because it was saved for important emotional and dramatic moments. Had we scored the obvious, it would have become like white sound [sound the listener doesn't notice]. You have to be stingy with music. Use it only where you need it. I'm a big believer that about thirty minutes of music is the maximum you should have in a film. Otherwise you get satiated. Yet the producer and director worry about it. If you haven't written enough for them, they snitch music from other places and keep putting it in, and it really kills the whole thing.

What financial constraints do you have in terms of recording time and the size of the orchestra you use?

GOLDSMITH: It depends totally on the budget of the picture. The last picture I had eighty-five men and I recorded for forty hours. The picture I'm going to do now, I'm going to have sixty men and record for eighteen hours. It's a great joy to have a gigantic apparatus in front of you, but I've had as few as five or six men and it's been a ball. Somehow everyone thinks of me as doing monstrous films and bombastic scores, although I prefer to do an intimate film such as *A Patch of Blue* [directed by Guy Green, 1965]. But there are certain demands in a picture. When you do a picture that has tremendous scope, you need tremendous scope in the music, too.

Is the instrumentation one of the first things you decide, or does that come later?

GOLDSMITH: Before I write, before I even get my thematic material, I figure out my basic orchestra. The orchestra is the composer's palette. That dictates everything else to me. I might want to write a score that's predominantly strings, such as *Chinatown*. After I saw the picture, I said immediately to Bob Evans [the producer], "I'm going to use four pianos, four harps, strings, two percussion, and a trumpet." He said, "Great." He didn't know what the hell I was talking about. It seems sort of weird, four pianos and four harps, but it sounded super. I don't know why, but all of a sudden I felt, "That's the color I want."

The trumpet was the main thing you were aware of. Bob kept talking about the period—Los Angeles, 1935. You see the period on the screen, so it wasn't necessary for me to comment on it, yet you wanted a bit of that feeling. Bob had fallen in love with a Bunny Berigan recording that had a trumpet. I used the trumpet and constructed sort of an old-fashioned theme, woven into very modern music. I was able, particularly in the main title, to have a fresh sound and yet give an indication of the period.

Are there some kinds of films that offer less opportunity to a composer than others?

GOLDSMITH: Some pictures I'm asked to score I say, "Forget it. You don't need any music." Certain pictures just don't need it. There is no rule. A film that is extremely heavy with dialogue generally does not need music, although I've done films that were practically all dialogue where music worked very well. *Freud* [directed by John Huston, 1962] was 95 percent dialogue, yet it needed music.

When I first talked to [novelist and director] Michael Crichton about *Coma* [1978], I said I didn't think there was any need to have music in the first half of the picture except for a bit of source music. There was nothing but exposition, and when you're just dealing facts and setting up plot there isn't much purpose to having music there, because it is not emotional.

Music is there to underline or heighten the emotional aspects of the film, whether the emotion be terror, love, hate, joy, innocence, whatever kind of emotion. I've been conducting and started to cry; I've gotten a chill up my spine, because all of a sudden it clicks. I am in control of that, and it's interesting that the film will heighten the emotion. You put the music and the film together, and you get an even higher peak of response. That's what's really exciting. I wanted to find the right time to strike in *Coma*; the second part of the picture was the first time we saw the villain, and that was the first piece of music in the film. It was maybe an obvious place but it was also the right place, because that was where the suspense started.

We all know that a film is much more successful when you

care about someone. It's the same thing for me as a creator—if I find a character I can identify with, it's less of an intellectual task for me. *Islands in the Stream* [directed by Franklin Schaffner, 1978] has probably had a deeper effect on me than any other film I've done. Perhaps I felt such an empathy with the Thomas Hudson character [played by George C. Scott] because I have four children and have felt the guilt that so many parents do as their children are growing up. That picture was in period, and it was a beautiful, broad canvas of the old style. The music had to be within the confines of the dramatic and technical scope of the picture. I could not get too sentimental over the Hudson character; there had to be a masculinity to my thematic material. Yet I couldn't be impartial. That was a great task, to find the basic material that nine-tenths of the score was built on.

I try to limit the music to one thematic idea, to sum up what the film is about. Everything else is an elaboration of that basic idea. In some films, such as *Patton*, you have more than one theme. When I sit down with a pencil in hand, I eliminate all the intellectual rationale and just start writing a totally emotional response. I often marvel over a period of four weeks—which is hardly enough time to write a score, but that's what we get nowadays—as I see the development of a simple idea.

How do you feel about the use of dramatic counterpoint?

GOLDSMITH: I don't know if any of you ever saw a picture called *The Wild Rovers* [1971], which was a beautiful film, one of Blake Edwards's best, before it got emasculated because of studio politics at MGM. The end was the classic chase of the good guy by the villains, and I thought, "Why does the music always have to be played *prestissimo* [as fast as possible]?" That was not the emotion I wanted. I wanted to play the fear of the man who is being chased, and the mounting tension until he gets killed. The music was very intense. At first everyone looked at me rather strangely, but it worked beautifully. That wasn't a formula, but the structure of that film impressed me to do it that way. It was not doing the obvious; it was not playing what you saw on the screen. I would call that dramatic counterpoint.

In the opening of the picture I used a honky-tonk piano doing some kind of old-time Western dance tune that I made up. Later, Ryan O'Neal was shot, and William Holden had to amputate his leg. It's a gory scene. I used the honky-tonk piano again, except I augmented the oom-pahs with an accordion and a banjo and a bass, and it got increasingly frantic in tempo as he was cutting off the man's leg and the camera moved closer and closer. I punctuated it with oddly placed, very dissonant, low brass chords, and above it a very intense string line, two pieces of counterpoint against all this joyous music. That's another example of playing against the scene.

Do you do most of the spotting [placement of the music] alone, or do you do it with the director?

GOLDSMITH: It's a give-and-take with the director. After you have conceptualized the overall approach, then comes the time when you have to be specific, and that's the spotting.

The first thing is the rhythm. Music is basically rhythm. And a motion picture is rhythm too, because it's going through the projector at twenty-four frames per second, ninety feet per minute; it's a constant, like a heartbeat. A sensitive composer has a great feel for the rhythm of a scene. I can tell by writing the music if a scene is edited well. There will be an easy flow of music. If all of a sudden the structure of a film is uneven, I will find the music becoming uneven and labored. Many times in the spotting of a picture I'll say, "If you give me more footage here, I can make a statement that will highlight that scene to a greater extent."

During the spotting, the music editor takes notes of where the music starts and ends. I may make a comment to the music editor that I would like to emphasize a certain point or that I'd like to drop the music for a few seconds and let sound effects play. He will then take that scene on a Movieola [a viewing and editing machine], break it down frame by frame, and give me a written description of the scene and the time, down to a tenth of a second. So I have more descriptions than any kind of a shooting script could ever have—all the dialogue, every movement—and you write to that. I also use a Movieola at home to back it up. The film has to be a fine cut. You are writing to such precise timing that if they take out six frames, which is a quarter of a second, it can throw everything off. But not everything is scored that way. If you have, say, a montage on a beach, just an atmospheric scene, you write a piece which would convey the general emotion of that scene very impressionistically.

When you're recording the music with an orchestra, the picture is projected on a screen and you use a clock. There are markings on every bar of your score to show how many seconds into it you are. And when you reach a certain point there will be a mark on the screen and a mark on your score so you will know to give a downbeat there. That's where you change the mood. We then go through the dubbing process, which is placing the music, the sound effects, and the dialogue and then mixing it all together. Those are the basic steps I follow as a composer.

In Patton, *when Scott is on the battlefield talking about Carthage, is that a spot where Schaffner had already decided he was going to use music, or was that your idea?*

GOLDSMITH: That was Frank and I. Frank wanted the music to start on the cut as Patton's jeep drove into the scene. That didn't feel right to me; I felt it was too soon. I felt that the moment it should come in was when Scott stands up, and all of a sudden you know he's almost been transported back in time.

I prefer to spot the picture by myself, have notes made, give them to the director, and then go back through it with him. Some directors don't come near the composer when he's spotting; others start with me right away. Some directors don't want to leave you alone for a second. The more nervous a director is about his film, the more he's going to shove in.

Is there much pressure on you to produce a hit tune or enough music for a sound-track album?

GOLDSMITH: We went through a period in the 1960s when motion-picture music was just a means of exploiting a piece of music for commercial purposes, and the dramatic values of scoring were secondary. But thank God the critics have finally begun to jump on people who think like that. I think we're coming to an end of that era, and young directors are going back to the idea that music in a film should be music for a film and not for a sound-track album. But I will try to write as melodic or pretty a theme as I can for a picture. There are popular tunes that come out of my pictures, but I didn't intend them that way. The way a score functions in a motion picture is not necessarily the way it functions in an album, so you sometimes have to restructure it. There was not that much music in the second *Omen* [*Damien: Omen II*, directed by Don Taylor, 1978], so I wrote additional music for the album.

I hate songs in pictures unless they have a reason to be there. You can't tell me that some silly song in the main title is going to make it a better picture. Why all of a sudden in *The Towering Inferno* [an Irwin Allen production, directed by John Guillermin, 1974] is a woman singing a song while the fire's going on upstairs? You know what it's there for—they wanted an Academy Award [the song, "We Will Never Love Like This Again," by Al Kasha and Joel Hirschhorn, did win the Oscar]. There's no other reason for that. The song in *Casablanca*, "As Time Goes By," really works. Because the whole focus of the scene is around the piano, the words, the music, the characters, the situation, the ambience of the whole thing works marvelously. But if they want a hit song, I tell them to get their number-one song composer and don't come to me.

What attracts a serious musician to film scoring?

GOLDSMITH: Terrific question. There are very limited opportunities for a concert composer. One can try to subsist on grants, which is getting more difficult all the time. One can go into teaching, but that was something I didn't feel equipped to do. And one can go into writing for films, which I wanted to do because I was always interested in drama. It is a marvelous experience to express oneself and grow. It eventually afforded me the kind of financial security that enabled me to write concert music.

The confines of a motion picture are certainly limiting to a composer. But on the other hand, over the years I have learned a technique and a discipline that I could not have learned had I not been scoring motion pictures. A great many concert composers could use the discipline and learn a bit of economy too. Motion pictures also enable us to experiment, if we are ambitious and daring enough. Don't forget, I can write thirty minutes of music and the day after I'm done I can start to record it with up to eighty or a hundred of the best musicians in the world, while a man can write symphony after symphony and during his lifetime never hear a note of it played.

Harry Horner

Harry Horner believes that people in show business should be generalists rather than specialists, and his own career is a case in point: he has been an actor, director, producer, stage designer, and, most prominently, a motion-picture production designer.

Horner won Academy Awards for his black-and-white design of *The Heiress* (1949) and *The Hustler* (1961), and was nominated for eight other films, notably the color film *They Shoot Horses, Don't They?* (1969). More than a mere set designer, Horner became involved in all phases of production, translating the story into visual images through the use of objects, settings, and color and costume coordination, as well as suggesting lighting and camera angles.

Born in Czechoslovakia in 1910, Horner first wanted to become an actor, but his engineer father insisted he also study architecture at the University of Vienna. During that time he directed and acted in student stage productions and studied with the great director Max Reinhardt.

When Reinhardt fled Hitler and came to the United States in 1935, he asked Horner to go with him to design the spectacu-

149

lar New York Central Park production of the Jewish-history pageant *The Eternal Road* by Franz Werfel and Kurt Weill. Horner said later, "If I had resisted becoming an architect when my father insisted on it, I probably would have wound up in an oven in Austria instead of coming to America."

Horner's career as a stage designer flourished with such plays as *Our Town* and *Lady in the Dark* and with operas for the New York Metropolitan Opera. Producer Sol Lesser brought him to Hollywood in 1940 for the film version of *Our Town*, on which Horner collaborated with the premier American film production designer, William Cameron Menzies.

Horner's film work showed the influence of Reinhardt and Menzies in his subtle combination of expressionism and realism. Believing that the film designer is a valuable collaborator with a director in helping tell the story, Horner did memorable work with such major directors as William Wyler (*The Little Foxes, The Heiress*) and George Cukor (*Winged Victory, A Double Life, Born Yesterday*).

Horner became a film director in the 1950s, though without notable success, on such films as *Red Planet Mars* and *Step Down to Terror*. He also directed and designed numerous plays, operas, and TV shows, and was producer-director of a Canadian TV series, *The Royal Canadian Mounted Police*.

Highly active in the past decade, Horner designed such acclaimed Los Angeles Music Center stage productions as *Idiot's Delight* and *Time of the Cuckoo* and numerous major films such as *Harry and Walter Go to New York, Audrey Rose, The Driver*, and *The Jazz Singer*.

SELECTED FILMOGRAPHY

1940 *Our Town*   1941 *The Little Foxes*   1943 *Stage Door Canteen*   1944 *Winged Victory*   1948 *A Double Life*   1949 *The Heiress*   1950 *Outrage / Born Yesterday*   1951 *He Ran All the Way*   1952 *Androcles and the Lion / Beware My Lovely* (director only) / *Red Planet Mars* (director only)   1953 *Vicki* (director only)   1954 *New Faces* (director only)   1955 *Life in the Balance* (director only)   1956 *Man from Del Rio* (director only) / *The Wild Party* (director only)   1958 *Step Down to Terror* (director only) / *Separate Tables*   1959 *The Wonderful Country*   1961 *The Hustler*   1964 *The Luck of Ginger Coffey* 1966 *Fahrenheit 451* (associate producer only)   1969 *They Shoot Horses, Don't They?*   1971 *Who Is Harry Kellerman and Why Is He Saying Those Terrible Things About Me?*   1972 *Up the Sandbox*   1975 *The Black Bird*   1976 *Harry and Walter Go to New York*   1977 *Audrey Rose*   1978 *The Driver / Moment by Moment*   1980 *The Jazz Singer*

THE SEMINAR

Harry Horner held seminars with the Fellows of the Center for Advanced Film Studies on February 19, 1970; October 11, 1971; February 3, 1976; and October 11, 1976.

What is the difference between an art director and a production designer?

HORNER: The only difference is that when you call yourself a production designer, you get more money. A production designer and an art director are the same thing. When I worked with William Wyler on the first film we did together, *The Little Foxes*, he said, "I don't know why there are so many directors on a film. *I* am the director. Why are there an art director and a director of photography? Why are there all these goddamned directors?" So I said I would call myself a production designer.

The man who invented the title of production designer was William Cameron Menzies [among his many films were *Things to Come, Gone with the Wind, Kings Row*, and *Around the World in Eighty Days*]. Menzies was *the* great production designer, the first one who thought that designing is not a matter of simply doing background decoration, but taking an active participation in the creating of the scene. I have similar beliefs.

A production designer should stimulate a director to see more than he has seen. By "seeing" I don't necessarily mean something visual: to understand more, to be more curious about a character, about a landscape, about the relationship between the setting and a character. The designer must not be looked upon as a specialist who only knows that when it is a Victorian room you have to have a round door and when it is a Gothic room you have to have a pointed door. The conceiving of a picture has nothing to do with decor per se. That comes much later and is really secondary. I find that I always look down on technical things. As a stage designer I hated scenery, because I found it an intrusive element. All great pictures and all great plays are in the writing, not in the designing, ever.

How did you make the transition from the stage to films?

HORNER: I was invited to Hollywood to work on *Our Town* [the 1940 film of Thornton Wilder's play]. I worked on the play in New York; it was done without scenery, only with props, and it made quite a splash. Thornton Wilder and the director, Jed Harris, had the idea that it would be interesting not to be burdened by the setting. Each person in the audience would envisage setting it differently anyway. I found this such an interesting device, such an interesting elimination of all that crap called scenery, that I thought we should do that in the film.

I went to Hollywood and I made literally thousands of sketches. The director, Sam Wood, finally said, "Harry, this is all too daring"—or "intellectual," "progressive," or whatever. He said, "You don't know anything about movies. You don't know what a dolly shot is." Mr. Menzies was engaged instead of me to design the film. He saw my sketches and said they were very good. This famous man insisted that he would share his credit with me, which was extremely kind. I've often wondered whether I would do it for another colleague. From then on I was the protégé of Menzies, and it helped me tremendously. But I hated *Our Town*. I thought I didn't participate enough in it.

How closely do you usually work with the director?

HORNER: I've had the luck to work with some of the giants, such as Willy Wyler and George Cukor. All great directors, though they are maniacs, can also be humble. Cukor is not really interested in camera setups. When I worked with him [on *Winged Victory*, *A Double Life*, and *Born Yesterday*], he would say, "Harry, *you* set up the camera." That is a difficult position. Naturally, the cameraman was worried, and stagehands would say to me, "Harry, *you* are directing the picture." I told that to Cukor, and he said, "Fuck 'em! I am getting the credit, so it doesn't matter who does it." That is absolutely the right attitude. Certainly I knew I wasn't directing the film. I contributed.

It is terribly important in a film to find this happy marriage between people. Unfortunately, there are many insecure people in this business. There are some directors who think that if they let somebody else do something their own position will be lowered. Only fools are jealous. Anybody who feels he can do it alone robs himself. The director is constantly faced with questions, with choices, and the designer helps him to make up his mind.

I'm also a director. I directed several films but, as you see, I did not stay with it, although I prefer to direct. For a designer, that is a good thing to do. We all should know as much as possible about each other's specialties, because, if nothing else, it widens the tolerance of one to the other.

Could you discuss a specific film and how you went about designing it?

HORNER: Let us talk about *The Heiress* [directed by William Wyler, 1949]. It was based on the novel *Washington Square* by Henry James. *The Heiress* plays primarily in a house. We did it at Paramount with all the facilities of a marvelous research department, which can help a designer put together a period—in this case, the 1860s.

I went to New York to get the feeling of the period. At that time you still could have photographed this on Washington Square; now there is nothing left of it. We all felt it would be simpler to handle if we shot it on a set. Washington Square Park was the back lot at Paramount, a set called the Boston Park. It was not as large as it seemed. I found in my research that in 1885 the park was a parade ground. It gave me a marvelous way to show the progress in time of the story—the parade ground later had a wooden fence, then they had gaslights and it became a park. This was not done so anybody would pay attention to it; most of the things one does are meant to have an instinctive effect on the audience.

I felt there were three functions the house should fulfill. When the father, Dr. Sloper [Ralph Richardson], looks at the house, it is like a shrine to the memory of his dead wife. She had marvelous taste, so the house should look terribly elegant. His daughter, Catherine [Olivia de Havilland], is just the opposite of her mother, shy and with no taste. He always compares his daughter with his wife; his daughter appears to be dumb and can't do anything except stitch. To the girl, the house is a cage. Whenever we photographed her, without spelling it out too much, there were walls. We also built a winter garden, a greenhouse, in the back with Victorian grillwork; when she goes to look for her lover, and it's raining, she's caught like a bird in a cage. And for her lover, Morris Townsend [Montgomery Clift], I wanted to invent scenes which would show the temptations of the house, where he would see the wealth. He is an adventurer, and it is never clear whether he really has any love for her or only impressed by the wealth of the father.

In Townsend's eyes, this house was the most marvelous castle that he wanted to possess together with the girl. On the street outside the house there was a shiny, elegantly engraved brass plate which said, "Doctor Sloper." It was attached in such a way that the first time we see him come to the house he stops there, and before he goes up the stoop he uses the brass plate as a mirror to fix his tie. It's a kind of natural symbolism. Little things suddenly matter.

There was a dining-room scene where he was invited for dinner. I thought it would be interesting if we would start the scene not at the dining table but in an anteroom where they kept all the silver, as the servants were bringing in the soup tureen. By showing all the silverware and all the glassware, we can see Townsend's reaction to the family's wealth, to a world that was desirable to him.

The staircase was a very dramatic effect. I designed it like the heart of a human being. It was the pivotal point of the house. I wanted Catherine to have certain feelings when she would go up or down the steps. There was a mirror placed on one of the landings, and you could see the rest of the house through it. To see her in the mirror when she rushed down to her lover gave the impression of extra speed. When she had to climb up at a moment of defeat—when she finally knew he was not coming to marry her—the climb was very dramatic. I thought the designer could help this by making a very steep staircase.

These are the things a good art director should give to a director. The director sometimes doesn't think of these things or doesn't have time.

Was William Wyler particularly good at finding uses for set and costume details during the filming?

HORNER: William Wyler was famous for allowing forty takes of a scene. After three takes, eight, twelve, you would say, "God, what else is there?" But he would count on accidents. When you do forty takes, actors will let go. There is a sequence in which Catherine comes down the staircase on her way out of the house, wearing a broad taffeta skirt and carrying a little tote bag. As she passes the living room she sees Townsend standing there, and she's so excited she is short of breath. She was supposed to show love, awe, and shock at his being in her house. Wyler didn't like it—he didn't know what to do with it, or he didn't say. Olivia de Havilland was desperate. She did it mechanically, and started to cry. Then she did it for the thirty-second time. She came down this steep staircase, which was my invention, and because she had done it so many times, she was nervous and she dropped the little bag. It slipped down her taffeta skirt, making a whistling noise. This was really what he wanted—an accident that was beyond acting. It happens after the actor becomes lax. The first twenty or thirty takes are really exercises to that moment in our subconscious nature when we do something that is unplanned.

When you work with a costume designer such as Edith Head on The Heiress, *is she brought in at the beginning of pre-production?*

HORNER: They want to save money, so people generally are brought in as late as possible. Edith Head came on when they thought they were ready. She had the advantage of having a lot of research already available. Had she insisted on another concept that was better, or more suitable to Wyler's taste, nobody would have contradicted her. Nobody is there to fight with anybody unless it is over something terribly important. The production designer should have his hand in all of these things, not as a matter of ego but rather of total style.

Could you explain how you do research, how you stimulate your imagination?

HORNER: It is terribly important to look at many sources of information. The first things I become interested in are the characters and their relationships with each other. The characters, naturally, are tied to a period: a Victorian group of people will act differently from a group of people who live in our time. I read the script and I make a list of all the things I don't know, all the questions I have: "How does a doctor live? How does he practice in the 1860s? Where does he practice? Does he go to an office or does he have an office at home? What does the office look like? What sort of instruments does he use?" Other things, too: "How would a wealthy man in this social milieu think? How would he talk?" This can come from the production designer. I compiled many research volumes for *The Heiress*, books of costumes and furniture and manners and other things. The more one knows about the period and the behavior of the people in the period the better, whether it is two years ago or a hundred years ago. I find that when I study the life of the people in a period, I can create an entirely different dimension. Sometimes it's heartbreaking, when you do not work with a sensitive director and you find that what you are doing not only is not appreciated but is not used. You know much more about the characters than an unprepared director who says, "I'll just work on my improvisation."

The research file on a picture is mostly text, not pictures. To me it's interesting to realize suddenly that something which seemingly is just research, just an unimportant detail, can be used dramatically. I did a film called *Harry and Walter Go to New York* [directed by Mark Rydell, 1976], which I thought didn't deserve its bad notices. I fared very well with the critics, but when they say the only good thing was the design, that's a very bad sign. Don't be happy if you are a designer to whom that happens. We shot all the scenes of New York streets of the 1890s here in Hollywood. Choosing the year of the story was left up to me; I chose 1893 because it was the last year when there were no automobiles on the streets of New York. One of the charms of the picture was that while we talk of automobiles as being noisy and smelly, people back then complained just as strongly about the noise and the smell of the horses.

I wanted to give the feeling of the big change at the turn of the century. That period was the time when New York broke up all the main streets, took out the cobblestones, and started to pave the streets with asphalt. Electricity was newly available, and there were telephone cables everywhere. Skyscrapers were starting to go up. I wanted that change because it was one way to avoid the cutesy-pie stuff that was in the sets I had to use from previous period productions.

Do you still do scene sketches when you are preparing a film?
HORNER: Yes, rough sketches to convey moods to the director. One contribution I made on *The Hustler* [directed by Robert Rossen, 1961] was in a scene that was to take place in the men's room of a pool hall. It was the scene in which Paul Newman's thumbs are broken, and we were to see the breaking. I felt that

it would be much more interesting to see it through the window, with his face distorted against the frosted glass.

There is a danger in having a production designer who plans every camera setup, as if to suggest that when they are put together they can become the film. You run the danger of limiting an impressionable director who can be intrigued by a visual effect rather than by the true development of the characters. Some directors fight against such careful planning. I've found it practical to sketch several versions. If the director says, "I don't like it," you can throw it away. It's cheaper to throw away sketches than to shoot the scene several ways and throw the film away.

Then do you sketch the actual plans for the sets?

HORNER: An art director or production designer is not supposed to make those sketches; there is another union, the illustrators' union, to make them. I disregard this. I must make these sketches; they are like piano exercises for a pianist. I make quarter-inch-scale drawings and give them to the draftsmen. You tell them you want the door done this way, but then you don't work on it anymore because you are now busy making sketches for the remaining sets. You make the ground plan, but otherwise you cannot really contribute to it.

How much influence do you have with the director once the sets are built?

HORNER: It depends on the director. It is a question of great diplomacy. The director and the cameraman are your friend-enemies. They love you when you make the schedule. However, when you look through the camera, the cameraman says, "Who is shooting this?" He'll say he can't shoot white; you have to paint it all gray. When you design for the stage the lighting is your prerogative. When you design for film, the lighting is the prerogative of the cameraman. With the director you have to be very tactful. With a man like Rossen, it is just as well to give him the sketch, to remind him what you have discussed with him the night before. Don't cry if he doesn't use it.

What problems do you encounter in designing a contemporary film such as The Hustler?

HORNER: The primary problem was the poolrooms. There were seven or eight in the story. We shot almost all of it on the sound stage, because Rossen said the pool shots—the trick work—

would be very difficult. It sometimes took thirty takes. Rossen
wanted to have total control of the locale; he wanted to take a
wall out when he wanted to, which you can do on the stage.

We wanted to do the film in color. I told him if he wanted
certain effects he might be able to get them better on the stage.
I thought it would be interesting to do the whole film in a mono-
tone, but to accentuate the green color of the tables, which would
inflict a sort of hypnosis on the viewer. We designed it that way,
but they finally decided not to spend the money for color.

The main pool hall was a location, a modern loft on 44th
Street in New York, which I redesigned. I used that loft because
it had thick walls and very good columns. My assistant, Al Bren-
ner, and I brought in thirty-six pool tables, put paneling on the
walls, replaced the cash register, and installed a coat rack behind
an iron fence. We shot there for three weeks, from eight in the
morning until nine in the evening. At night some of the cast
stayed there to practice. Rossen and I felt that a greater reality
would be achieved by doing the film within the limitations of a
real location. When you can't take out a wall you have a much
greater reality than when you take out a wall and the room is
twice the size.

In designing the poolrooms I made careful studies of texture. It disturbs me terribly to have a story that really happened
to people done on a phony set. A cracked door or a wall that has
the outgrowth of humidity on it is very difficult and expensive
to re-create, because it takes so much time. In Hollywood, you
have to watch out because when you want a crack in a wall, the
plasterer draws a crack on the wall, which looks like a crack
drawn on the wall. In New York there are artists who are superb
chemists, and when you say to them, "I want a door in a cheap
apartment where there is no upkeep; it has been painted over
several times with different paints and now it has cracked and
peeled," they will ask you, "How old should it be—fifteen years
or seventeen years?" They put acid and all kinds of things on it
and within a week it looks absolutely real.

The set of Piper Laurie's apartment in The Hustler *[she plays
Paul Newman's lover] was an effective representation of her character—traces of elegance in a general disorder. How did you approach that?*

HORNER: The search for a character is a fascinating experience which I recommend to directors just as much as to designers—to go around and find the person you are looking for, maybe not in one apartment and not on one street, but in many—how they live and whom they talk to and what the characters that surround them look like. Piper Laurie's character is a complicated one. She comes from a very good family. She goes to a course at the university twice a week. She drinks. She has no moral strength. She drifts around at night and takes in men. She is terribly lonely, a lost soul.

Now comes my problem. One doesn't know that kind of pad. I asked myself where she would live: probably in an area where there are students. I thought perhaps she might be a music student. If so, she probably would live on the West Side near Carnegie Hall between the Fifties and the Sixties. I went to boardinghouses where they rent flats to students. It was fascinating because of the human debris, old and young, who lived there. Sometimes I was frank and explained that I was doing a film. If the manager seemed inaccessible, I said I was looking for a flat.

I saw the place of a ballet dancer, a young girl who was very sloppy, and I made rough sketches. It was an interesting mixture, because she had prints on the wall which showed taste—Picasso, Miró, etc.—but she left clothes and books all over the place. To get to the toilet you had to go through the kitchen, and the bathroom door was always open because she used it as a wardrobe, with lots of clothes hanging there. Outside was a marvelous shiny corridor with locks that are replaced every time a new person moves in. You remember what that all spells. To repeat it successfully is another problem.

There were three rooms in the set for Piper Laurie's apartment. The problem was to design the middle room—the entrance room—in such a way that I could see into the bathroom, so that a dialogue could take place between Paul Newman in the bathroom and the girl in another room. The entrance to the corridor and the corridor itself were prominent, to give the feeling of the type of boardinghouse in which she lived. The door became a terribly important factor. Laurie's character is never secure. Newman's character is not reliable. There is the possibility that he may run away at any moment. This can be expressed visually: I designed the apartment so that many scenes could play near the door.

I twist a room this way or that, but I believe one should not overlook architectural reality. There are certain things the audience notices. When you place windows, you must know whether they can function architecturally. A door that leads out into a hallway can't have windows on both its left and its right. But I always remember, too, that it would be interesting to do something different. In this case the living room is a step higher than the entrance hall and the rest of the apartment. It gave me the possibility to be at a certain height with the camera, and to have Newman stand lower than Laurie and still have both faces together. It seemed realistic, too; it was one of those architectural monstrosities that happen.

In the final analysis, what can the designer add to a film?

HORNER: The designer can create a mystery. You might disagree, but I feel the mystery that is created by the designer is like the paintings of the Italian painter Chirico. He draws a street with shadows cast by sunlight coming strongly from the side and from behind the painting. This is the sort of mystery one should create in films. One should never be sure that around the corner there isn't the influence of another century or another character, some mystery that lies behind the scene and gives it another dimension.

Part of this dimension is the setting. When something looks beautiful, when the period is conveyed, when the mood is conveyed, then decor fulfills its function. Therefore I find that the process of my work is primarily emotional and not visual. Please, you directors, don't think that the art director is just a carpenter.

THE COSTUME DESIGNER
Edith Head

Few Hollywood craftsmen have become as well known to the general public as was costume designer Edith Head, whose seemingly ubiquitous credit appeared on more than a thousand films before her death in 1981.

Winner of eight Academy Awards (and thirty-four nominations) since the costume award was first given in the late 1940s, Head, with her elegant designs, epitomized the glamorous era of Hollywood in which designers sought to make gods and goddesses out of stars. One of the few in that period to work with both men and women, she designed for such films as *The Lady Eve, Double Indemnity, The Heiress, Sunset Boulevard, All About Eve, A Place in the Sun, Roman Holiday*, and *The Sting* as well as the Bob Hope–Bing Crosby *Road* pictures and many Alfred Hitchcock films.

An indefatigable and witty personality, she also appeared frequently in public to present her views on fashion. She was a guest on many TV and radio talk shows, a lecturer on the women's-club circuit, author of two books, and even appeared in two films (as herself), *Lucy Gallant* and *The Oscar*.

Born in 1907, Head taught Spanish and art before being

hired by Paramount in 1923 as a sketch artist for chief designer Howard Greer. Her association with the studio was to last until 1967, when she moved to Universal, where she was under contract until her death.

At Paramount, Head began costuming minor characters and moved up through low-budget Westerns into major productions. She worked as Greer's assistant until he left the studio in 1938, when she became chief designer. Among the many stars she costumed there were Gary Cooper, Cary Grant, Mae West, Barbara Stanwyck, Ingrid Bergman, Gloria Swanson, Dorothy Lamour, Ginger Rogers, Veronica Lake, and Shirley MacLaine. She also worked frequently with such directors as Preston Sturges, Cecil B. DeMille, Billy Wilder, Leo McCarey, and George Stevens.

Head's name first became famous with her costuming of Sturges's comedy classic *The Lady Eve* in 1941; her Spanish styles for Barbara Stanwyck created a fashion fad, as did her later designs for Elizabeth Taylor in *A Place in the Sun* and for Grace Kelly in Hitchcock's *Rear Window* and *To Catch a Thief* (her favorite among all her films).

Though best known for her high-fashion designs, she was one of the few designers with such a wide range, including Westerns, historical epics, and science fiction. Her most celebrated late work was for Paul Newman and Robert Redford in *Butch Cassidy and the Sundance Kid* and *The Sting*; her last Oscar nomination was for John Huston's *The Man Who Would Be King*, for which she designed forty thousand costumes.

The films for which she won Oscars were *The Heiress, All About Eve, Samson and Delilah, A Place in the Sun, Roman Holiday, Sabrina, The Facts of Life,* and *The Sting.*

SELECTED FILMOGRAPHY

1925 *The Wanderer* 1927 *Wings* 1929 *The Virginian* 1932 *Love Me Tonight* 1933 *She Done Him Wrong* 1935 *Ruggles of Red Gap | Peter Ibbetson* 1937 *Make Way for Tomorrow* 1939 *Beau Geste* 1940 *Christmas in July | The Great McGinty* 1941 *The Lady Eve | Ball of Fire | Sullivan's Travels | Here Comes Mr. Jordan* 1942 *I Married a Witch | The Road to*

Morocco   1944 *Going My Way | Double Indemnity*   1945 *The Bells of St. Mary's | The Lost Weekend*   1946   *The Blue Dahlia | Notorious*   1948 *The Emperor Waltz*   1949 *The Heiress*   1950 *Samson and Delilah | Sunset Boulevard | All About Eve*   1951 *A Place in the Sun*   1952 *Carrie | The Greatest Show on Earth*   1953 *Come Back, Little Sheba | Roman Holiday | Shane*   1954 *Rear Window | Sabrina | The Country Girl*   1955 *To Catch a Thief | The Trouble with Harry*   1956 *The Ten Commandments | The Man Who Knew Too Much*   1957 *Funny Face*   1958 *Separate Tables | Vertigo | The Buccaneer*   1960 *The Facts of Life*   1961 *Breakfast at Tiffany's | Pocketful of Miracles*   1962 *Hatari! | The Man Who Shot Liberty Valance*   1963 *The Birds | Hud | The Nutty Professor | Love with the Proper Stranger*   1964 *Marnie | What a Way to Go!*   1965 *The Great Race*   1967 *Barefoot in the Park | El Dorado*   1969 *Butch Cassidy and the Sundance Kid | Airport | Tell Them Willie Boy Is Here*   1970 *Sweet Charity | Myra Breckenridge*   1973 *A Doll's House*   1975 *Rooster Cogburn | The Man Who Would Be King*   1976 *Family Plot | Gable and Lombard*   1978 *Sextette*   1979 *The Big Fix*   1982 *Dead Men Don't Wear Plaid*

THE SEMINAR

Edith Head held a seminar with the Fellows of the Center for Advanced Film Studies on November 23, 1977.

Sometimes a movie such as The Great Gatsby *can create a fad in fashions, and department stores will feature the "Gatsby look" for months. Does the idea of doing that ever influence you when you begin designing a costume?*
HEAD: No, it's purely an accident. A dress I designed for Elizabeth Taylor in *A Place in the Sun* [directed by George Stevens, 1951] was copied by a line that did debutante party dresses. Paramount counted thirty-seven Elizabeth Taylors dancing at one party. A good costume designer should try not to do it. Everybody hopes to hit on something people like, but I'm too busy with the film to think about it.

There is no similarity between a studio designer and a designer who creates clothes to be bought. A commercial designer makes so many collections a year, certain price ranges, certain fabrics. And they usually do what they consider their own thing—"an Oscar De La Renta dress" or whatever it might be. However, in motion pictures we costume designers have absolutely no control over what we do.

We are given a script, and we have conferences with the director or producer and with the stars. What we do is create an illusion of changing an actor or actress into someone else. It is a cross between magic and camouflage. In real life, clothing is worn for protection, to look good, or whatever reason you like. In motion pictures, it's to help the actress on the screen give the impression that she is the person in the story. We have three magicians—hairstylist, makeup artist, and clothes designer—and through them we're supposed to kid the public that it really isn't Paul Newman, it's Butch Cassidy. We go through any kind of device we can to break the mold of the actor or actress. If it's an actress who is known for wearing a certain kind of clothes, we usually go to an extreme to break the concept. In a picture like *The Country Girl* [directed by George Seaton, 1954], we try almost to shock the public into saying, "Well, I don't believe that's Grace Kelly after all."

It doesn't matter so much with men, but with women we are able to work our magic, particularly in period films, changing their figures, making them over. The important thing is that we have the power through the medium of clothes of translating people into anything we want. That's why I think we're a very important part of the whole project. I like to think that if the sound went off, you'd still know a little about who the people were.

After you read the script, what are the steps you take in preparing for production?

HEAD: You break down the script into a wardrobe plot, in which every role is defined. You make little side notes, such as, "Ask the director whether he thinks it would help the mystery if she wore a hat with a veil in this scene." You take your costume plot and have your preliminary meeting with the director and producer.

When you work with a director, you immediately have to find out his point of view. You've seen films by Alfred Hitchcock, George Roy Hill, and Joseph L. Mankiewicz—well, all three of them are completely different.

If you ask Hitchcock what he wants, he'll say, "My dear Edith, just read the script." Hitch is the only person who writes a script to such detail that you could go ahead and make the clothes without discussing them. I do sketches for him, though. A Hitchcock script is so completely lucid: "She's in a black coat, she has a black hat, and she's wearing black glasses." That was Karen Black's character in *Family Plot*, the last one we did. A lot of scripts give no clues at all. When you work a great deal with a director you know his likes and dislikes. Hitchcock has a phobia about what he calls "eye-catchers," such as a woman in bright purple or a man in an orange shirt. Unless there is a story reason for a color, we keep muted colors, because he feels they can detract from an important action scene. He uses color like an artist, using soft greens and cool colors for certain moods.

When we did *The Sting* and *Butch Cassidy and the Sundance Kid*, George Roy Hill had done as much research as I had. In fact, he did more on some of it. He is a perfectionist. When you work with him day by day, it's as though he were another designer.

Mankiewicz I never met, because they borrowed me just to do clothes for Bette Davis. He called me and said, "I love your work. Just do what you think is right."

So you see, there is no rule. You can get directors who are charming, you can get directors who are completely uncooperative. Every time you work for a new director, you say, "I hope he's not terrible," because a bad director, a director who is not interested, is impossible.

Do you do sketches even if you are planning on using clothes that can be bought?

HEAD: When I go to see a director, I take a sketch pad and a pencil, which I stick in my hair, and as he talks, I sketch. I'll say, "Do you like this sort of thing, with a turtleneck sweater?" He'll say, "No, I see it with a low neck, with a scarf," so I quickly do that. Then I won't waste time, because I already know what he wants. I've discovered it's much better to communicate with the eye than with the ear. Most directors, producers, and actors and actresses like to see something drawn, even if it's just a pencil sketch. When you talk to people, it's hard for them to say, "I don't like it" or "I do like it."

A lot of directors today couldn't care less what material it is, or what color. I hate people who talk about the good old days, but that's the trouble. In the past, you had certain directors and actors with whom you'd work all the time. Many times now you work with people for the first time, and they don't want to discuss, they just want you to tell them.

What sort of budgetary constraints do you work under?

HEAD: In the earlier days, we had no real budgets. The wardrobe head would give an estimate to the budget bureau, but I never knew what I had to spend. In the old days if you made a dress and it wasn't any good or the actress didn't like it, you made another. Today we are budgeted. The budget comes before anything we design.

Also, in the old days every studio had its own stable. At Paramount I knew with whom I was working. I knew I had Grace Kelly, I knew I had Dorothy Lamour, I knew I had Bob Hope and Bing Crosby. You could plan, you could order fabric. But now I am working on a picture called *The Big Fix* [directed by Jeremy Paul Kagan]. There's an actress coming in tomorrow who will probably work on Monday. She is between a size 14 and a size 16. That's all I know about her.

The next film I'm going to do is for Alfred Hitchcock, *The Short Night* [Hitchcock became ill and Universal canceled the project after his death in 1980]; it's being shot in Finland and will be a contemporary film. But with Hitchcock, I will know in time who's going to be in the parts and whether we will buy the clothes or make them. It's the kind of picture where the girls wear sweaters and skirts, sports clothes. Ten or fifteen years ago we'd have made the sweaters and skirts. Nobody does that today, not even Hitchcock, because the whole financial picture has changed.

What kind of staff do you have on The Big Fix?

HEAD: In this picture, I'm doing the women. Richard Dreyfuss has a costumer doing his clothes. I have an assistant who helps me shop, and there are people who make the clothes. It's like a business, and if you're doing a huge picture, you have a lot of people working, but otherwise you have a small staff. In the past, a designer was much more important, because everything we did was made. Even if a star wore an old, ragged apron, you made it, because she was a star. Every designer in town was working. Today a lot of them are unemployed because we are doing so many films that are contemporary. Today's pictures are mostly men. There are very few women's pictures, and the women's pictures are mostly character pictures. In the past we made all men handsome and all women sexy and glamorous. Now we just buy them both a pair of blue jeans!

We don't have time and we don't have the budget. But still you should have a designer work with you. The director and producer can come and say, "I want to get a little character—I want the man to look a little shabby" or "I want the girl to look a little seedy and tough," and you can do a great deal to help them. I even work with writers when they describe a costume or want to know what will help motivate the story.

The trouble is that while you have to have a cameraman and you have to have an art director, you don't have to have a costume designer on a film. Very few of the designers have permanent jobs, because we don't have a union. Actors can bring in their own clothes. Or somebody goes out and shops. There isn't much chance of being a designer now.

Could you give us some idea of how much time a costume designer would spend on a film today, assuming it's not a period piece, and compare that with how much time you'd spend on a contemporary picture some years ago?

HEAD: Well, on a Hitchcock film today, we have from two to eight weeks to prepare. On a Cecil B. DeMille picture, such as *The Ten Commandments*, we had fifteen months to three years to prepare. Today we're trained to work faster. I have a crew who will work twenty-four hours, and I could make a dress overnight if I had to do it. Nobody would know it was done so quickly.

How long did it take you to design the costumes for The Sting *[directed by George Roy Hill, 1973]?*

HEAD: We dressed all the principals, about six of them; we made about sixty costumes. It took six weeks, because I had to show George Roy Hill all the fabrics. This doesn't happen very often with directors, but he has a tremendous interest in everything. I like working with someone like that. Also, it's easier working with two male stars [Robert Redford and Paul Newman] than it is with women. When in doubt, dress men. They're not as involved in what they like and don't like. Women have favorite colors, favorite necklines, they like belts, or they don't like buckles. Men are not as fussy. You get a Redford, a Newman, or a Cary Grant and you can do anything with them because they are athletes, they have wonderful physiques. You get somebody who is bottom-heavy or top-heavy, and you've got a problem.

Do you ever buy clothes off the rack? And if so, do you have any stores you favor?

HEAD: You don't go to Saks to buy blue jeans for people in jail. But if I buy blue jeans for a leading lady who is very elegant and chic, I go to Saks. I do a great deal of shopping with stores that will let us take things out on approval. A lot of stores do not want to be bothered with our taking out a lot of clothes and holding them until we have fit them. We know where to get things, but there's usually a time element involved, trying to get it in time to shoot. Sounds hysterical, doesn't it? It is.

Can you explain how you integrate your work with that of the production designer?

HEAD: Half the fun is working with a production designer who has the same feeling toward the material. I show him the sketches before I even show them to the director. I'm married to one, incidentally [Wiard Ihnen]. I think that unless you synchronize the color of the room with the color and pattern of the costumes, it's impossible to do a coherent job of designing. People have been caught doing a blue nightgown in a blue room, in a blue bed, with blue pillows, and you can't tell who's who.

Do you find that the costumes you've designed have a lot of influence over what the colors of the film will be?

HEAD: No, the production designer has more choice of the color concept. He rules things. I don't think we've ever had any great conflict. I also work with the cinematographer. It isn't as bad now, but before color we had a great problem because there were certain things they wouldn't shoot. Some of them wouldn't shoot dead white and certain colors. I discuss it with them if I have a pattern that I think might jump or be dizzying. Certain plaids and checks are treacherous. I know most of them by heart, but when in doubt, always ask. At least when you present your sketches you know there's not going to be trouble later.

Do you work with the hairstylist and makeup person as well?

HEAD: I show them the sketches.

So many times in the films of the '30s or '40s, it seems the costumes are perfect, and yet the makeup and hairstyles are not.

HEAD: During that era, the stars had so much power that they would sometimes wear their own hairdos, and it would be completely wrong with the clothes designed for them. I send the hairstylist and the makeup person the sketches, so they'll know, for instance, that it's going to be a high collar, and they won't give her long hair. It's a courtesy between departments. I'm not sure that other designers do this. To me, it's self-preservation.

How can you make sure a costume will be practical in terms of the action demanded in the film?

HEAD: When Bette Davis was fitting for *All About Eve*, she suddenly threw herself onto the floor. We thought somebody had stuck a pin into her, or that she was having a fit. But there was a scene in the picture where she had to throw herself down, and she wanted to see if the dress would work. So whenever I fit an actor or actress who might be rough on the clothes, I have them perform that action in the fitting room. That's why my fitting room is so large. And if there is any possibility of a change of action, I have the director or the assistant director come and watch the second fitting. It's that important.

Many actors do not begin to internalize the character until they see what they look like. Laurence Olivier is a great one for going from outside in, and he likes to see his costumes. Is that true of the actors you've worked with?

HEAD: Of course it is. Practically all performers want to see themselves in costume. In front of a huge mirror, with special lighting, something instinctive comes over actors and actresses. I believe you should allow an actor or actress to discuss and criticize before we get on the set, and say, "I cannot wear this because I cannot do that." Occasionally you get someone who double-crosses you on the set and says, "I can't wear this—it's too tight," but not very often. Actors and actresses in earlier years were much easier to work with than some of the contemporary people who think they know all about everything. The young actresses of today are not nearly as easy to work with. They are concerned with what they like. You have an actress who says, "I don't like pink, I don't want to wear pink." Well, who the hell cares? I get so mad at them. I never had this with a great star, ever.

Do you have to be concerned with the sounds different materials make?

HEAD: I used to, but not so much anymore. Still, you have to be careful of beads that have a metallic ring when they fall against each other, you have to be careful about certain types of jewelry, and you don't use much taffeta. It's particularly difficult doing period films, because you have these great taffeta hoop skirts with multiple petticoats making rustling sounds. You can do it deliberately. In *The Heiress* [directed by William Wyler, 1949], there was one scene where Wyler wanted to hear the rustle of Olivia de Havilland's skirt as she came down the stairs. We used taffeta, and they put the sound camera quite close so you heard the rustle. We can control sound; we can control practically everything.

William Wyler is also a perfectionist. *The Heiress* was set in two periods, the mid- and late nineteenth century. We had crinolines and we also had hoops, which is a slightly different silhouette; most directors wouldn't care. But there were scenes where Olivia de Havilland was seen dressing, and we had her in petti-

coats, with the little corsets and corset covers. Wyler even sent me
to a fashion institute in New York that had a great collection, to
be sure that every button and every buttonhole was absolutely
accurate. If I had to say which picture I did that was absolutely
perfect, it was *The Heiress,* because Wyler insisted on it.

Period outfits are so complex because it isn't just a costume,
it's the hat, it's the hairdresser, it's the wig, it's the jeweler, it's the
gloves. I did a picture last year called *Airport 1977* [directed by
Jerry London], and Olivia de Havilland had to wear a black silk
coat and black suede gloves. I could not buy a pair of black suede
gloves in Los Angeles. They said, "Madam, we don't sell them
anymore." I had a pair of my own that I let her use.

*How did you get started? How did you discover that what you
wanted to do was to design costumes?*

HEAD: I taught school in La Jolla a long time ago. I have a
theory that once you've taught, you can do anything. When I was
teaching, I didn't have enough money during the summer, so I
had to get a job. There was an ad in the paper: "Wanted: Sketch
artist for Howard Greer, Paramount Studios." I was just starting
at Chouinard Institute, and I borrowed a lot of sketches. I had a
fantastic portfolio, with seascapes, landscapes, portraits, costume
designs. Howard Greer said, "I have never seen so much talent in
one portfolio." I got the job. The next day when I wasn't good at
drawing, he had a sense of humor about it. I don't advise you to
try that. It never occurred to me how dishonest it was until afterward. But I worked as a sketch artist and an assistant for many
years.

Would you say that people now are as trained as you were?

HEAD: No. I worked with Travis Banton and Greer, who were
top designers. For years they would do the stars, Marlene Dietrich
and Claudette Colbert, and I would do the grandmothers, all the
aunts and relatives. I did all the horse operas. I'm an expert on
horse operas.

In the Cecil B. DeMille pictures, we would have seven designers. I would do maybe Delilah, then we'd have somebody else, say
Dorothy Jeakins, who did the men's clothes. Then we'd have a
designer who did the horses, because in DeMille pictures the
horses were very important. When you were working with seven
designers it was lovely.

The only trouble I ever had with DeMille was working on his elephant pictures. When I do interviews, everybody asks, "What is the worst time you ever had?" Really, it's been not with people but mostly with animals. The first animal I ever dressed was an elephant. Nobody told me that elephants eat leaves. We had great blankets made of flowers and grapes, with leglets of roses, and the elephants ate practically everything. Animals are interesting. I also had trouble with the snake in *The Lady Eve* [directed by Preston Sturges, 1941]. A snake is, as you know, all in one piece, and they wanted us to design a little necklace with a bow on it. Every time she wiggled away, the bow stayed behind.

Have you done any stage work?

HEAD: *The Pleasure of His Company* was the last stage production I did in New York, and that was rather pleasant. Theater and motion pictures are completely different. In the theater you have to project to the highest balcony; detail has to be broad enough to carry through an entire theater. You also have to do clothes that last, in case the company goes on the road. In pictures, if our dress collapses after one night it really doesn't matter. In film we are shooting for the close-up. Marlene Dietrich once stood for eight solid hours fitting a beaded dress: "Now this bead will go over here, and this bead we'll move over there." We lost two fitters. They collapsed, but she didn't. In the picture everything on her beautiful beaded dress was in the right place. In the theater it wouldn't have mattered.

Do you do extensive research on period films?

HEAD: Most designers like myself have worked on so many films that we automatically know those things. In the early days there was no such thing as complete accuracy. I did a picture once in which one of the actresses was crossing the prairie from the East Coast to the gold rush in a prairie schooner. We had a buffalo stampede, three Indian attacks, and a prairie fire. And every morning the heroine came out with white ruffles and her hair done up in curls. Nobody cared, because the public accepted motion pictures as a fantasy and an amusement. We used to give the women low-necked dresses with the bosoms hanging out, and I'd say, "But don't you know, they didn't wear low-necked dresses in the old days?" The producer would say, "My dear Edith, if everybody had worn high-necked dresses, you wouldn't have been here today, because there would have been no sex."

But today we have found that the public is much smarter—they read more, or they look at more television—and I'm usually pretty careful, because we get insulting letters saying, "They didn't wear that material then." And do you know that in the old days you could show a man's navel in a picture, but not a girl's navel? In all those pictures with Hedy Lamarr we used to stuff pearls in the dancing girls' navels or give them diamond belts. But Victor Mature and all the men went around in little shorts with their navels exposed. I could never figure that out. The censorship was very funny. You could have a girl in a white slip—that was all right; but if it had lace on it you couldn't show it, because that was sexy. But it was much more fun in those days.

You did a picture called The Great Race *[directed by Blake Edwards, 1965] in which every time Natalie Wood appeared, she was wearing a different dress. Was that the kind of film you like to costume?*

HEAD: Wasn't that lovely? That was the most fun because it made no sense at all. Another one was *What a Way to Go!* [directed by J. Lee Thompson, 1964]; every time you saw Shirley MacLaine, she had on a different dress. It wasn't a good picture, but it was fun doing the clothes. Those days seem to be over.

THE CASTING DIRECTOR
Joyce Selznick

One of the most respected casting directors in Hollywood, the late Joyce Selznick was trusted by producers and directors to do much more than simply present names of prospective actors for smaller roles. She conducted talent searches for many lesser-known actors and actresses who rose to stardom through her shrewd instinct and drive.

Selznick, who died in 1981, came up with such offbeat casting coups as Gary Busey for the lead in *The Buddy Holly Story*, Kurt Russell for the title role in the TV movie *Elvis*, former model Jessica Lange for her acting debut in *King Kong*, and then-newcomer George C. Scott for his career-building supporting part in *Anatomy of a Murder*.

Among other young actors whom Selznick helped launch were Faye Dunaway, Ann-Margret, Candice Bergen, Tony Curtis, Telly Savalas, Cicely Tyson, Harvey Keitel, Colleen Dewhurst, Jessica Walter, Godfrey Cambridge, Joan Hackett, Albert Brooks, Rob Reiner, Billy Dee Williams, Dick Van Dyke, Bo Derek, Ann Jillian, and Tommy Lee Jones. She also tried, without success, to sell Robert Redford and Barbra Streisand to the studios before they became important names.

177

Born in 1928, Selznick was a cousin of producer David O. Selznick and a niece of the Warner brothers. Originally intending to become a writer, she started as a secretary at Warner Brothers after graduating from Hollywood High School at fifteen. Within a few months she became a continuity writer, translating books into provisional screenplays, but an opening in the casting office sidetracked her.

At age seventeen she decided to try it on her own in New York City as an actors' manager, and it was there she made her first discovery, a young actor named Bernie Schwartz, whom she groomed into stardom as Tony Curtis. But Nate Spingold, executive vice-president of Columbia Pictures, suggested she learn more about the film business, and he sent her on the road to promote films, an experience she found invaluable.

After running the merchandising department of the newly organized Screen Gems TV syndication company in New York, she was chosen at age twenty-six by Columbia president Harry Cohn to be East Coast talent head for the company. She developed many new stars during that period, also taking on the duties of story department head, making her one of the most powerful women in the industry.

In 1967 she became head of the worldwide talent and story departments for Paramount Pictures in Hollywood, where she helped develop such films as *Downhill Racer* and *Rosemary's Baby*. She left to help package and produce the 1974 black film *Claudine* and to become an independent casting director. Besides casting films and TV movies, she also cast James Komack's TV series *Chico and the Man* and *Welcome Back, Kotter*.

A year before her death she finally achieved her ambition to become a writer with the publication of a novel, *Blue Roses*.

THE SEMINAR

Joyce Selznick held a seminar with the Fellows of the Center for Advanced Film Studies on February 8, 1978.

How much power does a casting director actually have over the casting of a film?

SELZNICK: There are two kinds of casting directors. There are casting directors who submit lists of people whom they are familiar with and leave casting decisions pretty much to the producer or director. They take a rather passive course. On the other hand, I'll give you a case in point, but I will not tell you the name of the picture because that would not be fair. I cast a picture a few years ago, and in reading the screenplay I saw that the leading character wasn't finely etched. I thought we should not cast it the way it was written, because if we did we were going to end up with exactly what we had on paper: an uninteresting character.

How do you compensate for that? By casting an actor who will add a dimension to the part. I went through an enormous fight with the director, writer, and producer. The actor I wanted to use was Richard Dreyfuss, who was unknown then. Whether you like Dreyfuss or not, Dreyfuss is a character, a very individualistic actor. Had he played the role, that picture might have succeeded. The actor they went with was exactly the actor required by the script. The picture failed very badly.

I'm not arguing whether I was right or wrong about that, but unless they have enormous confidence in you, it is hard to change the minds of most directors and producers. If you do, then you become a really creative casting director. It almost becomes a producer's job. For the most part, a casting director is the victim—or the hero, as the case may be—of the selections made by the producer and the director.

Jerry Wald, a big producer in this town, once said, "It takes talent to know talent." The really talented men and women in this business know talent. They respond to it. Those who do are the winners because casting does make a great difference. Unless you have that sense for talented people—not just good actors, but those who can project excitement onto the screen—the actors are going to water down your effort.

What's an example of a film in which you were successful in persuading them to cast a role unconventionally?

SELZNICK: I've just completed a film like that, *The Buddy Holly Story* [directed by Steve Rash, 1978]. The original idea was to find a musician who could act. I said, "No, let's find an actor who is a musician." I happened to know that Gary Busey, whom I had cast in many films, was a first-rate rock-and-roll guitarist and singer. That was his hidden ambition.

This picture was started two years ago [as *Not Fade Away*, with Jerrold Freedman directing] but was canceled during production. I was the casting director, and I had a full-out war with the director about how to cast it. I wanted Gary to play the role. Gary is a tall, tow-headed, fair-skinned blonde; he looks about as much like Buddy Holly as I do. The director had no imagination whatsoever. He hired some young man from England with a guitar.

Another group of people got hold of this material, came to me, and asked how to cast it. I said, "You've got to do it the way I tell you," and they listened. Columbia just bought the picture. The way Gary Busey plays the role, you would swear he was Buddy Holly come back to life. With his hair dyed and with the glasses on, he looks incredible, and he is a fine actor, a great musician. With Gary I put Don Stroud, whom nobody in this town knew, to play drums, and a boy named Charlie Martin Smith, who plays a pretty hot bass. The three of them together are Buddy Holly and The Crickets. Buddy Holly died when he was twenty-one years old; Gary Busey is almost thirty. How do you take a thirty-year-old guy and have him play a fellow who was still a child when he died? All you had to do was to match the three actors together. They are all in the same age range, and you will accept it. You will believe Gary Busey is Buddy Holly. That is the license you take in casting when you are allowed to cast the way you want. Some directors you can give three actors, but many directors are not satisfied unless they have seen every actor in town. Then they are *really* mixed up. They always think they're missing something. They aren't. There are very few really fine actors in this town. There are a lot of exciting personalities.

Most of the time this is what happens. Let's say you've got the part of a seventeen-year-old Italian boy, a street boy. What you do is take the best of the director's and producer's image of the part as they've explained it to you and try to fit it with the best actor who comes close to that image. You bring the actors in and they read. Then it's just a question of weeding out until you get down to those the director likes best, and he makes a decision. If he's not satisfied with the first fifty or a hundred seventeen-year-old would-be gangster boys you bring him, he'll want to see another two hundred and fifty of them. He can make you crazy. He may end up casting a blond Norwegian who's nothing like the character.

I read that after Freddie Prinze died in 1977 you were given only two weeks to find a replacement for him on [the NBC-TV series] Chico and the Man. *Where did you find Gabriel Melgar, the little boy you cast?*

SELZNICK: On the street. We had examined probably every Latino schoolboy in Los Angeles. With children you primarily look for spontaneity and naturalness; you don't want them to have training. Except in rare instances, a child actor doesn't get better as he grows older and gets experienced, because he usually loses that marvelous natural excitement. After having those children read, I decided to continue searching for some kid who had the charm we were looking for. I went down to Echo Park [a Latino neighborhood] one Sunday afternoon, and there were a lot of boys walking along the street. I approached them. First of all, they were suspicious. Second, most of them weren't terribly interested. But within maybe a half second of talking to Gabriel Melgar I knew he was the boy.

There was a lot riding on that choice, wasn't there?

SELZNICK: No, because I didn't think I would make the wrong choice, after having looked at hundreds of boys. We couldn't continue that show with a stand-in for Freddie Prinze. No one could be against an authentic little twelve-year-old boy, but from time to time in the beginning even he was very pained by some rude letters that said, "You're not Freddie Prinze." The poor kid didn't know how to handle it. You do wonder whether you do people a favor when you do this.

After you found him, did he have to make a test before getting the part?

SELZNICK: Yes. I would have said, "Let's go with him," but I'm afraid that the network had something to say in the matter. The producer and the director are maybe not as quick as I am to say yes or no. Usually they like to see something on film. Unlike most casting directors, I don't look at film. I don't believe in it. I don't want to waste my time sitting looking at actors on film. If I'm going to cast a young man as the czar of Russia, seeing him play a cop on the corner is not going to tell me anything. I like to depend on what I feel from the reading or from the interview. In fact, there are certain directors I won't even work for if they have to see a piece of film on every actor who comes through their door, unless there's a problem about how someone will photograph. But for a performance, it is not necessary. I don't think you will find many people who will admit to that.

What kind of sensitivity or natural ability does one need to recognize talent or the appropriateness of someone for a role?

SELZNICK: My approach is different from that of most casting directors. I spent every night for ten years at the theater. To me talent is very exciting. I get a kick out of being able to spot people, just as somebody who is attracted to horses gets turned on by a thoroughbred. I would go anywhere. I did. I used to go out in the summer and spend eight weeks in my little Triumph, going to practically every summer-stock company when summer-stock companies really were the breeding ground for so many young people.

Sometimes I just found people who came to my office. Telly Savalas came in one day and I put him in three pictures immediately in New York. He had done nothing. I feel responsible for starting his career.

When I first went to New York I found Tony Curtis walking on a street corner, 57th and Broadway. I approached him and took him to my office. His name then was Bernie Schwartz. Everybody said, "Why, Joyce? Why him?" He was a little stout, he had a dialect you could cut with a knife, and he was hardly what you could call a trained actor. I would have bet my last dollar that he would be a star. It took about two years to launch him, but I cast him in a film called *City Across the River* [directed by Maxwell Shane, 1949]. I put him on the screen for about five minutes and told them, "Let him play himself and you will have a star." That is exactly what happened. He had the most fan mail on the Universal lot within six months after the release of the film. Then, of course, he couldn't talk, so they didn't know what to do with him. They put him in a picture called *Johnny Stool Pigeon* [directed by William Castle, 1949], in which he played a deaf mute. They figured, "We'll see what happens." The fan mail continued. Those were the days when we still could build stars.

Faye Dunaway I saw in the last act of *Hogan's Goat* at Lincoln Center. I was more impressed with her after I invited her to my office just to talk. Within fifteen minutes I decided that she was going to be a star. I am very proud of that. That is hardly a put-down of her ability on the stage, but something happened in the close interview that was very exciting.

I don't know how other people do it; I only know how I do it. It is mostly instinct, love of what I do, and sort of a sixth sense, I suppose. Then there is the hard analysis of an actor: knowing who has studied, who is equipped to do what. I would rather go with a child who had no experience, but I would not necessarily take that attitude with a boy of seventeen or a girl of twenty-one, although I have done that too. Everything has its requirements.

You cannot put an unschooled actor on the stage, because he won't make it. That takes years of training. On the other hand, you can take someone totally unschooled and untutored and put him on a television screen. I've done that. I found a young man by the name of David Hasselhoff waiting on tables, a marvelous-looking boy. I sent him to a coach, Lyn Weston, for what I call "instant training," because I knew of a spot for him on a CBS soap called *The Young and the Restless*. Lyn was a marvelous coach. He went to read two days later and got the part, and has since developed into a fine actor. The soap opera became, for him, the training ground that young actors used to be able to get in the East in the stock companies, in the theater, and also the kind of education they could get by doing "B" movies back in the '30s and '40s and '50s when studios still had their stock companies. Now television provides that climate for education for a lot of actors.

John Travolta proves it beyond a shadow of a doubt. He spent four years in the ABC series *Welcome Back, Kotter*. There was a time when most actors looked down their noses at the idea of spending time in television, because they thought it would spoil them for films. After four years of being a supporting character on *Welcome Back, Kotter*, Travolta ended up a superstar. He got visibility from that show. So the situation has changed enormously for people who want to be actors. Television has become a star-making vehicle.

I do think I understand what makes careers. I'm not just talking about actors; I'm talking about the vitality and energy and need and creativity in anyone who seeks an outlet in any of the creative arts. Whether you want to produce, write, or direct, or whatever your ambitions are, there are certain qualities you have as an individual that usually are a dead giveaway. You can't always be sure what part luck and one's ability to stay with a career play in it. You can't always predict what will happen along the way. But people manifest success. You can usually pick that up by talking to them for any length of time.

Have you ever made any mistakes?

SELZNICK: I've never been wrong in predicting that an actor would make a living in the business. As far as predicting a career, it depends on the degree. On the one hand there are a Candy Bergen or a George Scott, and on the other there are actors who have made a good living but have never gone to the heights I would have liked to see them reach.

How do you go about interviewing people?

SELZNICK: Because of my excitement in discovering new people, I keep a fairly open file. I will see everybody—they don't necessarily have to come from agents. I can tell a lot from a photograph. I'll "read" the people I talk to, and I can usually tell very quickly what their potential is.

I had a girl come in to see me about a year ago. I was looking desperately for the right girl. When I gave her something to read, she read only three lines and I said, "You're hired." She thought I was absolutely crazy. I do that, particularly with comedy.

After I conduct the initial interviews, we get into the reading sessions with the producer or director. I'm always there.

What do you talk about in the interview? Do you talk about the script?

SELZNICK: No. I'm interested in the résumé, particularly if it has a believable theatrical background. I'm not terribly interested in whether they've had television or movie experience. I like to know with whom they've trained. If they haven't had any training, that's all right; we'll see what they can do from there. But when an actor comes to me with training, I'm intrigued.

Do you let actors study a script overnight before they read for you, or do you prefer cold readings?

SELZNICK: I get more out of cold readings. I would never trust the full performance of an actor in the office. That is amateur time. A really good actor, one who knows his trade, gives you just enough to interest you and leaves something that the director or the producer can get later, when he's really into the part. I take into consideration that people are bad cold readers, but that's compensated for by the interview you've had before.

Let's say that the actor takes the script home and has it all worked out. Then he comes in and it's not what the director wants. He's lost the part. So it's best for the actor to work from instinct, because then the director has the privilege of saying, "No, I would rather have it this way."

Undoubtedly you have discovered actors who aren't right for what you are casting at the time. Do you look for something else for them?

SELZNICK: I'll give you a case. A young girl came to see me by the name of Candice Bergen. She was extremely beautiful and trained as a model. Very bright. She was ambivalent about acting. So I said, "Let's have you make a screen test. If you like yourself on film, you can decide whether you want a career." She made a test for a picture called *The Chase* [directed by Arthur Penn, 1966]. That test was about the best piece of film she's ever had to date. They didn't use her in the film because they felt they needed Jane Fonda with Marlon Brando. While I was working for Columbia, I sent that test to Sidney Lumet, who was directing *The Group* [1966, from the novel by Mary McCarthy]. I thought that Candy was perfect for the part of Lakey. He thought so too, and that was the beginning of her career. If you see something interesting in an actor, you try to find ways to move them into opportunities. It's called career building.

When you cast King Kong *[the remake directed by John Guillermin, 1977], what led you to cast Jessica Lange, who was a model at the time, as the female lead?*

SELZNICK: We tested about a hundred and fifty girls from all

186 THE CASTING DIRECTOR

over the country. Jessica Lange had no experience, but when she tested she had something on the screen that was necessary for the role: her total naiveté, that wide-eyed innocence. Some good actresses made their tests ludicrous by the way they acted with this huge mechanism called King Kong. They were not playing with the ape; they were playing with Robert Redford. When we sent for Jessica from New York, she thought it was a joke. She played her test with the attitude of "Why am I here?" We had her do scenes in which she was pleading with the ape in the forest, and she said later that she stood there feeling totally vulnerable. It was that vulnerability that was necessary to play the role.

Do you ask people about their past work?

SELZNICK: No, I'm not interested. I'm interested only in how I feel. Everybody's entitled to make career mistakes. That doesn't necessarily mean they're not good, nor does it mean that they shouldn't have another chance. What happens to most actors today is sad—they are considered as good as their film. Unless they're in a runaway hit, whereby their exposure to the public is so tremendous that they become known overnight, they can forget it. If they're in a film that doesn't make it, even with good notices, they start their career over again. They look for the next picture that's going to do it for them. I've seen that happen to a lot of actors. But television can give them a fresh start. I can give you a good example—a fellow by the name of Peter Strauss, who had had several leading roles in films. His career was going nowhere. All of a sudden came the ABC miniseries *Rich Man, Poor Man*, and his career was off and running. Nick Nolte, who was also made into a star by *Rich Man, Poor Man*, was around this town for years. Television, with its enormous projection, has created big stars, which is what the movies used to do. Television has brought back the personality syndrome. There's no question that television will bring us closer to the star system than at any other time in the last twenty years.

What often happens in films is that it is so hard to get films made, and there are so few bankable names, that a producer or director will go to the first bankable actor who is available, whether that actor is right or not. It becomes a vicious circle, because in order to get his picture off the ground he makes compromises he shouldn't make. I'm not standing in judgment on this, because the person he wants might not be available for four years,

and then what is he supposed to do? He does the next best thing.
How valuable for an actor are Hollywood acting schools?
SELZNICK: Most of the schools I know of "teach" you camera
techniques and how to hit the mark, and they "teach" you how to
give a cold reading. I don't know whether they teach you acting.
It's all technical. There are only one or two coaches in this city I
would send actors to. Generally I would say, "Go back to New
York for that kind of training." This town is not theater-oriented.
I am still hung up on that, because I think it is basic discipline.
To be a fine actor takes a lot of discipline.
*Could that be one of the reasons an actor may start off with a blaze
and then doesn't continue? Because he or she doesn't have the discipline?*
SELZNICK: There's no question about it. The worst part about
it is that very often those actors who get a "break" are very unhappy because they don't have any kind of internalized sense of
their ability. They're never prepared for their break, so they're
always unsure and frightened. If an actor is not prepared and does
not constantly train for the work he does, he is like a doctor who
practices but never bothers to look at a textbook again. A lot of
his patients die. That holds true whether you're an actor or a
writer, almost any profession.
*If you are given a role to fill, how do you put the call out? Does
your office put the call out to all the agents in town, or do you
make specific calls to agents you know, for actors you know?*
SELZNICK: There's a convenient service that tells agents almost
every day what's around. If I'm casting something, I usually send
my information to this service. But most agents know when you're
casting and they stay in touch with you, or you will call them.
Some casting directors only see certain agents. It's easier for an
actor to get a job than an agent in this town. Very often actors are
stranded out there without any help. Unlike New York, where
anybody from the street can come to a casting call, here it's very
hard to get in to see a casting director unless you have an agent.
*I have a friend who has this exact problem. He's a very talented
actor.*
SELZNICK: It's a desperate situation for an actor to find an agent.
This is not a put-down of agents. They have to make a living. It
takes an enormous amount of spadework to take beginning actors

and go through all the beginning motions of introducing them to casting directors and getting them their start. It's very painful, it takes a long time, and it costs the agent a lot of money. So for the most part, agents don't like to fool around with unknown people. It takes so long that by the time they've made all of those steps to get an actor started, he has already gone off to another agent.

But you will take people who are unrepresented?

SELZNICK: I have. I've seen those people, and then I tried to get them agents. I find it very difficult.

Is it true that you tried to get Paramount to hire Jack Nicholson in 1967, and they wouldn't go for him?

SELZNICK: I was worldwide head of talent at Paramount at the time. A friend of mine asked me to look at an underground film for the purpose of introducing the producer to the studio. I looked at the picture, which was just short of a porno. All I could see was this fellow who knocked me out. At the end of the showing I said, "Who is he?" The producer didn't want to tell me, because he was interested in my buying his film, not in my hiring the actor. I had somebody else find out who it was.

Two days later Jack Nicholson came to my office. It was fascinating, a typical Hollywood story. He had been around a long time. He had done everything from directing to making films like that, and was ready to throw in the towel. He said, "I'm giving it three more months. I'm getting out because I've got a family and I just can't make a living in this business." I tried to sign Jack Nicholson to Paramount Pictures. I did not get very far, that is true. Three months later he ended up in *Easy Rider* [a Columbia release, directed by Dennis Hopper, 1969]. I didn't have anything to do with getting him *Easy Rider,* but I had the instinct about him. Jack Nicholson didn't surprise me a bit when he became a star. I knew that once he got a break he would make it.

Do you have any thoughts about the failure of talent? A lot of stars fail during their careers.

SELZNICK: Very often the ones who succeed are not those who work just in terms of their ability, just on stamina and personality, but those who have managed to organize their lives like businessmen or businesswomen. The fact that some fall off that plateau is often based on some kind of personal problem. You can say, "Well, there were no pictures" or "Maybe they didn't get the right parts," but there's always a way to stay on that plateau. Bette Davis is a good example. Even though she's in her seventies, she still performs. She has found a way to make the move. She loves to work. You do it best if you love it. If you don't love it, you lose interest quickly, and you look for something else to do. I believe there is always a place for a fine actor in this business.

THE INDEPENDENT FILMMAKER
Stan Brakhage

The major figure of the modern American avant-garde film, Stan Brakhage has created a dazzling body of work that is both intensely personal and broadly influential. Also an important theorist and teacher, Brakhage literally has changed the way filmmakers and audiences see the world.

Brakhage's goal—as stated in his 1963 credo *Metaphors on Vision*—is to enable people to use their faculties of vision in a creative rather than a passive manner, to see the world without social and cultural conditioning. Toward that end, he has restlessly transformed the material of his own experience into unique patterns of light, color, and rhythm.

Though sometimes considered difficult because of their unconventionality, Brakhage's films, as he observes with deserved pride, have been responsible for many innovations that have eventually been absorbed into the cinematic mainstream. The personal nature of his work has also encouraged many filmmakers, both avant-garde and commercial, to explore their own feelings on screen.

Born in Kansas City, Missouri, in 1933, Brakhage has spent most of his life in Colorado. He now lives in Rollinsville and supports his filmmaking by teaching at the University of Colorado in Boulder. He formerly taught film history at the School of the Art Institute of Chicago, and for several years made occasional industrial films, TV commercials, and other commissioned work.

Brakhage made his first film, *Interim*, in Denver in 1952. He studied cinematography at the Institute of Fine Arts in San Francisco, and during the 1950s he also spent time in New York City, where he came under the influence of such leading underground filmmakers as Willard Maas, Marie Menken, and Maya Deren. In New York he made one of his most important films, *The Wonder Ring*, an impressionistic portrait of the Third Avenue El.

With *Anticipation of the Night* in 1958, Brakhage advanced the close scrutiny of ordinary life and "moving visual thinking" that has characterized his later work. He has frequently involved his wife, Jane, and their six children in his films, such as the memorable film about childbirth, *Window Water Baby Moving*, and his epic about family life, *Scenes from Under Childhood*.

Other key Brakhage films include *Dog Star Man* (1959–64), a landmark of experimental cinema that has been compared to *Finnegans Wake* in its kaleidoscopic style; *Songs* (1964–69); *Sexual Meditations* (1970–72); and *The Text of Light* (1974), a study of light refracting through an upper-story window in a skyscraper. His work in recent years has become increasingly abstract, with series of short films identified simply by Roman and Arabic numerals. Though he has worked in 16-millimeter, most of Brakhage's films are shot in Super 8; they are truly "hand-made" works.

SELECTED FILMOGRAPHY

1952 *Interim*   1954 *Desistfilm* / *The Way to Shadow Garden* 1955 *The Wonder Ring*   1956 *Flesh of Morning*   1957 *Loving* 1958 *Anticipation of the Night*   1959 *Wedlock House: An Intercourse* / *Window Water Baby Moving* / *Cat's Cradle*   1961 *Thigh Line Lyre Triangular*   1961–64 *Dog Star Man*   1961–65 *The Art of Vision*   1963 *Mothlight*   1964 *Songs*   1965 *Fire of Waters*   1967–70 *Scenes from Under Childhood*   1968 *The Horseman, the Woman, and the Moth* / *Lovemaking*   1970 *eyes* 1970–72 *Sexual Meditations*   1971 *The Act of Seeing with One's*

Own Eyes 1972 *The Riddle of Lumen* 1973–80 *Sincerity/ Duplicity* 1974 *The Text of Light / Aquarien / Hymn to Her / The Stars Are Beautiful* 1975 *Short Films: 1975* 1976 *Short Films: 1976* 1977 *The Governor / The Domain of the Moment* 1979 *Creation* 1979–81 *A series of films titled with Roman numerals* (I–IX) 1980 *Murder Psalm* 1980–83 *A series of films titled with Arabic numerals* (1–18)

THE SEMINAR

Stan Brakhage held a seminar at The American Film Institute on July 21, 1972.

Do you have any kind of script before you begin a film?
BRAKHAGE: It's different for every film. Maybe it's best to take *Anticipation of the Night*. It was made fourteen years ago, when I was living alone in a little suburban house. Having been defeated by New York City, I had gone back to Denver, where I was raised. I was in a gloomy frame of mind, feeling that my whole childhood, as I remembered it, was an anticipation of death. Here I was, twenty-four years old; I had been making films since I was seventeen, and there was no acceptance of them, no place to show them. I was finally reduced to making a living by working for the Martin Missile Company on top-secret stuff, all of which was questionable whether it should exist on earth. I envisioned myself as having prepared to die, spiritually, and be a worker for the rest of my life. That being totally unacceptable to me, I was unconsciously and definitely contemplating suicide.

One day someone gave me a rose. It was very beautiful. I was disturbed by things that seemed to have no purpose, no intrinsic value in my life, but were beautiful all the same. In time this rose really was annoying, but it would have been ridiculous to throw it out, so I began to photograph it. Then all kinds of ideas sprang into my head. I have been involved with the flower my whole life long, and it took on special meaning when I was sixteen or seventeen and I read Gertrude Stein's poem "A rose is a rose is a rose." That poem has been despised and made fun of by practically everybody, but Gertrude Stein wisely said, "This may be true, but do I have to point out to you that it is the most often-quoted poem in the English language?" Let us go into the poem a bit, because this shows how my mind works.

In mythology, the rose essentially is a sex image, and I recognized from reading poetry that what you got from Gertrude Stein's three-time repetition of the word was: birth, sex, and death. I always rolled the poem around in my head—*a rose is eros is arrows is sorrows*—you can turn the wheel endlessly. I was also very involved in baroque music at that point in my life, and *Anticipation of the Night* is a baroque work. I remember that when I sang in the choir as a teenager we used to make jokes about Handel having twenty-five "hallelujahs" in a row. That's ridiculous—why couldn't he say it just once? As I grew older I came to see the majesty of it; Gertrude Stein helped me with that. Her poem reminds us of what Handel certainly knew—that there is no such thing as repetition. When you say "hallelujah" the second time it means something quite different from what it meant the first time, and so forth.

Then other ideas came that had to do with my sense of futility and wanting to deal with children. This film is, if you like, a prayer in the midst of despair. You live in these American suburbs and they are as repetitious as hell. You drive along the streets and here come the streetlights—*hallelujah, hallelujah, hallelujah.* Or when it's raining, the windshield wipers—*whap, whap, whap.* It's five o'clock and the sun is down and it's time to water the lawn. Denver is a city that prides itself on its trees and lawns. If you let your lawn go to seed, the neighbors get upset. So every day I had to water my enormous lawn.

My friends had just had a baby, and they set him loose on my lawn. He began crawling around, and I was out there watering. Suddenly I got the camera and started taking pictures of the baby. At this time of my life I was incapable of taking anything in life for granted. I had to create it out of light. I couldn't just take pictures of a baby on a lawn; I had to go up close and create that baby. I had to start with mounds of out-of-focus flesh imagery to get the movement of crawling long before you knew what was crawling. Then you see an arm, then part of a back, then a head, then the whole thing evolves and you have a baby.

After several weeks I began to make a kind of script, the only type I'll make—thematic, writing down certain themes that were occurring to me. The title came first, as it often does in my work, then all the things that occurred to me about the rose. I mostly use scripts to get rid of ideas. I did another type of scripting when I began editing the film. There were thousands of feet of film, and it was very complex. I had what you could almost call a musical score—scribbly lines representing a Greek temple or maybe just a circle for the streetlights, then an arrow pointing in which direction to go, so I could cut back and forth among directions of movements. When I'm actually editing, I have to throw that away, because the film is much more subtle in the way it behaves than I could ever write.

Your comments about the lawn indicated an interest in metaphor and in a kind of narrative. Commercial feature films seem to be moving away from storytelling; I wonder if this is a coming together of the avant-garde and the commercial film? They are not as far apart as they used to be.

BRAKHAGE: Well, they are. But the Hollywood film has taken many forms of grammar from the art film. For instance, I believe I invented the interruptive flash-frame in 1959, in a three-minute film called *Cat's Cradle*. What that means is that you have a shot and you interrupt it with a flash of something that has been or will be. It's a memory device: memory comes to you in flashes at first and finally establishes itself. This grammar was taken up and developed by Gregory Markopoulos, who made *Twice a Man*. Then it was used to jazz up television ads. They would show a flash of a cigarette, then another flash, and finally they would show you the cigarette. It's still used quite a bit that way. The first Hollywood film I know of that used this technique was *The Pawnbroker* [directed by Sidney Lumet, 1965; the film actually was made in New York, but is "Hollywood" in the sense of being commercial]. In a very short time it has become a normal, accepted technique, using the grammar as I used it and as Gregory Markopoulos used it.

This goes on continually. I could give as many as two dozen other examples from my work alone. I could give examples from Kenneth Anger and other filmmakers, but it would sound smart-alecky to say, "The artists are giving Hollywood its grammar." My childhood, like that of Gregory Markopoulos and Kenneth Anger, was saturated by Hollywood movies. The first movie I ever saw was *Snow White and the Seven Dwarfs* [the 1937 Disney cartoon feature]. Most of us still go to Hollywood movies and enjoy them, so we are borrowing possibilities from the Hollywood movie all the time. It seems at times that we are getting closer together, but we are not, because the absolute division is the overall purpose of the work.

The purpose of the Hollywood film is to help us all share in the same cultish dream; it is our tribal dance. The artist is always trying to create a new dream.

Occasionally there are artists who manage to work through studios in Hollywood and in Europe. Robert Bresson [the French director of *The Diary of a Country Priest, Pickpocket, Au Hasard Balthazar*, among others] is an example. He is to Europe what Orson Welles is to Hollywood. Here you get a type of fluke, a man who manages to make his particular level of art as if it were, superficially, an entertainment movie. One of the problems an artist has working in a studio is that he is always accused of being a dictator, and everyone hates him. He gets tossed out quickly, even if his work is a financial success. Most of the men we came to recognize as artists struggled with the studio. Many of them were forced to become actors to make a living. It's almost the final punishment Hollywood could put upon them—to make Erich von Stroheim [director of *Greed* and *Foolish Wives*] "The Man You Love to Hate." In Europe it's not quite so bad. Bresson probably never will be beaten out completely, as they beat Orson Welles out of Hollywood, but he too has an awful time raising funds for the next film.

A Hollywood film is a collaborative production. Other people are telling you what to do, and they are making all your decisions for you. You are an attachment to the machine you are operating. Many people feel comfortable with that slavery. I have made my living for years making commercials, and when I make one I prefer that they tell me exactly what to do. The problem is not only that it leads to slavery, but that there is an intrinsic lie involved, because it is not a process of trying to get a reality, but of trying to get an image that will be shared by the greatest number of people.

The major drive in making a Hollywood movie is to get a large amount of money back. Therefore they make a tribal dance that shows us the nightmares and dreams and aspirations of our society. That seems to me a perfectly authentic use of money, one of the most magical uses of money I know of in society.

I have to work with no regard for money. I must use whatever means I have and not go beyond them. I must not cry or stop the film because I can't buy an Arriflex [a professional camera]. In fact, I have on a shelf a stack of flip cards for the possibility that I may run completely out of money and can't buy a roll of film. I take Crayolas and make flip books, which cost very little. In the last several years, I have been able to spend a great deal on film— *Scenes from Under Childhood* cost me $20,000—but in that same period I also made films that cost me almost nothing. Someone will give me outdated film, and I already have the equipment, so I just have to make a print for $100. Money must not interfere with my considerations; otherwise I would start doing what Hollywood already does so well.

I feel that you trust yourself immensely, since your view of reality has to come from inside yourself.

BRAKHAGE: Not so. I'm always suspicious of myself. It is one hallmark of someone involved in the arts that he is extraordinarily unsure of himself. I don't know if I have succeeded or not. I don't know if it is fair after less than a hundred years to say that we've achieved an art of the film. The intention is there.

One of the important things is that if you are sufficiently interested in a film, it should hold up in an infinite number of viewings, with no waning interest. The price you pay is that it is tough to get into the first time, because it is so dense. An artwork always looks strange until people learn the rules of its newness. It is difficult at first, but it is the most tangible way to get at a reality.

I know that most of you must be involved in the narrative film. Often my contemporaries and I are attacked or scorned because it is said that we are not involved in narrative, and that narrative is the only true art. I think narrative is intrinsic to any continuity art. There is always a story in my films, but it may be a different sense of story from that of a normal Hollywood film. In the case of *Mothlight* it was important to me that I tell the story of the birth and flight and death of a moth. This is an intricate story; if you were to write it down, you would have a short novel. *Fire and Water* has a story like a detective novel, a story of heat lightning in a small neighborhood. At first everything is mysterious and difficult to comprehend; then you get a shot of one of the houses suddenly in daylight, and a strange sound, which to most people sounds like a dog whining frantically in a backyard. The sound really is the speeded-up cries of a woman in childbirth. *Fire and Water* deals slowly and cautiously with the essential terror in this small home, just as in a detective novel Raymond Chandler can make a room vivid to the imagination and every time you return to the room more of its intrinsic terror is revealed.

There is no war between the possibilities of an art and the possibilities of a tribal dance. If people make war out of them, it is because they feel that one is criticizing the other. I have no criticism of the Hollywood film, any more than you do. One of the great things about the movies is that you go to them exhausted with all of your problems, and for two hours you are Gregory Peck fighting battles and riding off into the sunset. If he is hurt, you feel hurt; he is you. That is the level on which it should be approached. I need that experience once or twice a week. It is a cheap drunk. It is relaxing and essential to my mental health. There are times when I will drive forty miles in a snowstorm to get to a goddamn movie, any movie.

The work of art is filled with things that hook the attention, but the attempt is to have them in such a balanced and intrinsic form that they do not suck someone up body and soul. I know very well that if I show a shot of a naked woman in a film, it is going to seduce men. Therefore, the best I can do is to counter that with something else which will effect a more balanced relationship with that image. My films are a little impervious at first; they exist totally by themselves on the screen. This offends many people, because they are so used to the delightful experience of being sucked into the screen and having the movie tell them what to feel. They feel they are being put down by the film that doesn't. This is a contradiction in our society, because if there is a film that could be the least involved in putting people down, it would be the film that leaves everyone in the audience free to be in his or her own skin.

A lot of people think you have to work hard and chip away at that image up there. Quite the opposite is true. It is just a world in itself, occurring. It is relaxed, open. Go with it.

Your film Window Water Baby Moving *is extraordinarily beautiful, and it was one of the first films to show birth so vividly. How did that film come about?*

BRAKHAGE: There were a number of medical films, but they disturbed me. They made people faint, and they showed birth as the most disastrous thing that could happen to you. Usually in black and white, with black blood coming out. I felt that this didn't give an image that was the real feeling at birth. That was one of the guiding impulses to make the film.

The practical reason we got into that film was that my wife, Jane, wanted me to be there when the baby was born. At that time, fourteen years ago, no hospital would permit it, so she thought that if I posed as a filmmaker they would permit it. They wouldn't. So the doctor agreed to come to the home with a nurse and certain emergency equipment. That is how the film came to be made.

Who was the photographer?

BRAKHAGE: I was. But Jane took the pictures of me. I had someone else work the camera in the scene in which we are kissing. The camera had been set up for weeks waiting for the baby to arrive. I knew so little about birth at that time; I had been to classes, but I had no experience of it. Finally came the night when Jane went into labor. I turned on the camera and realized there was nothing to photograph, so I went and kissed Jane. If I had plotted that, it would have looked phony.

For all I knew, having a baby was like being hit by a truck. This is the male view of having a baby. Much to my surprise, at the instant the child was born, Jane asked for the camera and took shots of me. I think my delight over the child in the film was actually a filmmaker's delight. I was astonished that she was photographing me completely unmasked.

Did you ever find your role as filmmaker clashing with your role as father and husband?

BRAKHAGE: No. I clutched at my role as filmmaker. It was all that held me together. This is often the case. Most of my filming is of some terror or joy that I cannot experience unless I am filming it. Otherwise I would come apart or run away. Life tends to be too much for me. My answer to that is to grab a camera. Then I begin to see it and develop an understanding.

I am always trying to share my films with Jane and the children, so that we can discuss them and learn more about them. *Scenes from Under Childhood* was born out of my desperate attempt to understand my children's world. It is a bad slip of the tongue to say "my" children; it implies a possession that isn't real. At that point there was a serious clash between myself and the children; I was either seeing them as cute or I was seeing them as problems. That was a miserable relationship. The situation became so desperate that I was forced to try to understand their world.

The only way I had to get at that, as honestly and as closely as I could, was to remember what I saw when I was that age. That led me to looking at them playing on the floor, and trying to remember what the floor looked like to me when I was down on it. Then it led me to photograph them playing on the floor in some way that had to do with my memory. You can see how desperate my struggle to understand their world was, because it was a $20,000 film, took seven years to make, and is three and a half hours long.

A big mistake that a number of people have made is to ask why I didn't put the camera on the floor. It was important to me that the camera be at my eye level. At times I do get down on the floor, but the camera is still higher than the children. All the images of the children and their activities in the house are seen through the eyes of an adult attempting to see the world in some relationship to them.

Why did you make Mothlight?

BRAKHAGE: I have formed a metaphor with moths. The moth beats himself to death against the light. That is what I have been doing all of my life. At the same time there is an ecstasy about their death: they are after the light. So, after years of watching their movements, I had the desire to pay homage to their death dance, but more than that, to understand it. The other thing I had noticed was that these little creatures fly in patterns. When you translate the patterns into musical terms, they become baroque. Their flight goes well with Bach.

My intention was not to kill anything when making that film. We took moth wings from around the lamps where the moths had taken themselves to die. I arranged moth wings, flies, gnats, mosquitoes, flower stems, and petals on tape; then I laid another piece of tape on top of them and printed them at the lab. It was a very tricky process. It took eight months working continually to make this three-minute film.

In watching your films I am moved not only by the visual metaphors, but by the rhythm. Do you consciously work for a rhythm in editing, or is that more intuitive?

BRAKHAGE: If I had the choice I would be a poet. I just did not have the obsession with language that it requires to be a great poet. But poetry and music mean much more to me than film. I spend my life with them. As much as possible, I try to get all the useful qualities from either of those arts into my work. You have to remember that Mercury is the god of both artists and thieves. Artists are always stealing things and then transforming them through their own processes into something new, which is not far removed from stealing a car and changing the license plates and repainting it so that you have a new car.

Why do your films include edge-flares [overexposures from the beginnings and ends of rolls of film]?

BRAKHAGE: In *Loving*, almost fifteen years ago, I took footage of a young couple in a passionate embrace, and it came back edge-flared. At first I said, "Oh, shit." Then I realized I had a perfect metaphor for the heat of their passion, so I used it. From then on I would use edge-flares whenever there was a use for them.

The drive is to make it honestly a film. That is one reason I scratch the titles onto the films: you start people off with an intrinsic sense that this is a film, not a window. I will stick a tripod leg in there or an actual image of the camera when I feel I have gone almost to the point of creating a Hollywood film, and that people might start being sucked up into the screen. In *Wonder Ring* you have a subtle but clear image of my own face. I'm always excited when I can use something that says "This is film."

Your films seem to have a great freedom of movement in the shooting, rather than the Hollywood preoccupation with making it perfect.

BRAKHAGE: I am involved in the study of the eye. I can't think of any other filmmaker who has really dealt with how the eye works physiologically. I feel that *Anticipation of the Night* and *Scenes from Under Childhood* are getting close. My dream would be to make a film which has all the qualities and kinds of sight in equal proportions, the way they exist in a day of normal living.

There are so many different kinds of sight. There is even one that is a little related to the Hollywood movie; what it lacks is the jumping around of the eyes to put a scene together. Cubism was an attempt to capture in paint the qualities of seeing. Isn't it true that things overlap each other as you see them? As my eyes dart around, the angles of your body and the way the light falls on you are completely displaced. Even when we think we are stony-eyed and staring at one spot, the eyes jump continually and the brain flickers a variety of interpretations of this one spot. I have increasingly worked with that quality of seeing. The problem is that most people are reading these films out of the trained experience of the normal film. So the film is making a statement to them that the person is jumping and leaping, while what I am stating is that the *eyes* jump and leap. This is what Gertrude Stein meant when she said that Picasso was the first painter in several hundred years to paint what he really saw.

But there is a great difference between the way something is shown on the screen and the way you actually see things. A hand-held camera, for instance, can make you sick.

BRAKHAGE: There is nothing in a film that really *is* seeing. Every artist attempts to isolate one aspect, whatever is fascinating him most at the moment. One important aspect is this leaping, moving quality of the eye. Of course, the hand-held camera is only an approximation of it. But when you get into a jam—in a fight, for instance and you need heightened seeing, you will find that your eyes behave more like a hand-held camera than like a still camera or a slowly moving camera. It isn't that your sight changes, but you become more dependent on consciously recognizing that flickering and using it. In art we only attempt to isolate moments. Imagination is the closest to reality that we can ever recognize.

I think of my films as documentaries. I never fantasize. I have never invented something just for the sake of making an interesting image. I am always struggling to get an equivalent on film to what I actually see.

I have to honor my forms of seeing, which are different from anyone else's. The artist usually has some kind of crisis with reality which is so intense that he or she has to start from scratch. If what this person creates is true enough to itself, it sticks and starts being shared by a few other people as a new vision. Then in a hundred years it becomes culture and we all share it together. Culture is the accepted imagination of one human being. You have to use that word imagination carefully: that is our most tangible reality.

What do you consider the role of the artist in society?
BRAKHAGE: Given that they are equally good people, I don't think an artist is any more important than an advertiser. Calling someone an artist is a fact, not a value judgment. It is unfortunate that people place dead artists on pedestals, because they use those statues to beat the living artists to death. They are always giving artists honorariums, which means they are not going to pay you.

The Museum of Modern Art offered to give me a complete retrospective of my work. They told me that I was the first independent filmmaker to get a complete retrospective, and I was only thirty-nine. They told me I should be either sixty or dead to get this great honor. They came on with all of this, and then they told me they weren't going to pay me any rentals for the films.

So I said no. Then they began to threaten me by saying that they could give this honor to someone else. Letters went back and forth. I finally said, "Look, I don't want your honors, because it will make the janitor hate me. Pay me the same as you pay the janitor, show my films, and praise him for keeping the hall clean. Because I have had too much praise and not enough money." To me artist means the same as electrician, plumber, garbage collector, doctor, what have you. It is a thing which is needed.

Short Subjects

KIRK DOUGLAS, actor-producer

"A movie has to be entertaining—otherwise you're a fake. The statement is secondary. It's the by-product. I could say I'm going to make a movie about how you should be good to your mother and father. Well, that's a nice statement, and we all agree on that, but it could be a dull movie. I don't care whether the movie's out of the Bible, or Shakespeare, or whatever it might be: you have to come up with something that holds the audience's attention.

"I can't overstress the danger of a filmmaker thinking, 'I want to make a statement. I want to be profound.' It's a piece of celluloid that somebody comes and looks at for two hours. Charlie Chaplin's a genius, but at the time he made his films nobody thought he was a genius. Laurel and Hardy—who thought there was any genius in that? There can be genius in entertainment, and there can be dullness in trying to be profound. Be able to laugh at yourself a little bit. Don't take yourself too seriously, and don't think your movie will revolutionize the world.

"You can sometimes say things in an oblique way. The danger is in saying something too directly. I get a kick out of seeing *Lonely Are the Brave* [produced by and starring Douglas, directed by David Miller, 1962] studied at universities. I think, 'How come Universal treated it like it was just a cheap Western?' Well, they didn't see it. Sometimes people look and they don't see. But, nevertheless, *Lonely Are the Brave* is not an arty-farty picture. If someone doesn't take any message from it, he should still be able to enjoy it; a ten-year-old kid might enjoy it on his own level. That's what I think is important."

ROBERT RADNITZ, producer

"What depresses me is that I care enormously about film and what I think it can do, but when I look around today, nine-tenths of the films I see have no feelings, no social meaning whatever. The more you attempt to make a film on a serious subject, the more you're going to get kicked, and the more difficult it is to make that kind of film.

"There was a period a few years ago when it looked like the personal film might be coming back. It isn't now. If you're going to make a personal film, you'd damn well better be making it with somebody who is big box office. How do you reconcile your artistic side and your practical side? Artists have always been in that quandary, and I don't think that it will ever change. But right now, in our industry, it's worse than it's been for a long, long time. Strangely enough, in the past year I've seen more interesting things on what used to be everybody's whipping boy, television, than I've seen on the big screen."

DAVID PUTTNAM, producer

"The number of questions that have to do with money in film-making classes frightens me to death. Because I don't give a monkey's nut about money, as long as I can stick a sandwich in my mouth and my kids are going to school. I can't believe my luck, that I'm in a business that allows me to pursue my hobby. And it does frighten me how many of you are obsessed by how much money is spent in advertising a film, how much money people have made on a film, how much they're going to make on the next film. It's something fundamentally rather unhealthy.

"I think you have to question your assessment of what is a successful picture and what isn't a successful picture. You must question the thinking in the industry that a successful film is a big-grossing picture. There are dozens of ways of making a successful film. A successful film can be a small picture that launches a tremendous actor. Think of the talent that was launched out of *Mean Streets* [directed by Martin Scorsese, 1974; written by Scorsese and Mardik Martin, and starring Robert DeNiro and Harvey Keitel]. Warner Brothers lost a lot of money on *Mean Streets*, but God knows the film industry owes quite a debt to the film. *The Duellists* [which Puttnam produced] launched Ridley Scott [the director], it brought Albert Finney back into film, and, strangely enough, with cable it will become a successful film in this country. It will break even. I'll never see a penny on the picture, but I'm enormously proud of it."

IRWIN WINKLER, producer

"One of the best reasons to do a film is when everybody tells you you shouldn't do it. Because if you stick to formulas, you're usually doomed to failure. You should go after material that is original and innovative. How many times did they tell me and my partner, Robert Chartoff, that films about fighters don't work, that women won't go to see them, that they have no overseas potential? And would you invest in a film with an unkown writer-actor named Sylvester Stallone [Chartoff and Winkler produced *Rocky*]? When everybody tells you there's not a chance in the world, that's the one you should go after."

ROUBEN MAMOULIAN, director

"One of the generals said that the worst tactical mistake a general can make is to underestimate his enemy. The worst mistake you can make is to underestimate your audience. You have to look up to them; you have to take for granted that they are just as smart as you are, maybe even smarter. If you carry that out, believe me, you always come out right."

PANDRO S. BERMAN, studio executive-producer

"Right now, obviously, the director is running the show. That was the case in the early days of filmmaking. There were no producers; D. W. Griffith and the other early directors were producer-directors. At a certain time in the history of the film business, things began to change. There was a time when the producer was supposed to be a creative man, not just a businessman.

"Louis B. Mayer [head of MGM] was responsible more than

anyone else for what was called 'The Producer System.' With Irving Thalberg [production chief], he set up a method which he felt could save a lot of money. He held the directors in check financially by giving the producers authority. He made them responsible for finding the properties and developing the screenplay with the writer. It may seem ridiculous to you today, but often under Mayer's system at MGM the director would be called in two weeks before the production started.

"If producers were intelligent enough in those days, they would delegate a lot of their authority to a bright director. I hope I was smart enough to let George Stevens and John Ford and the other top directors carry the ball. The only contribution I could make to *The Informer* was to supply Ford with $15,000 to buy the story. I always believed that a picture should be the result of one man's feeling and thinking, whether he be a writer or a director or a producer. I never believed it should be messed up by giving too many people too much of a say."

WILLIAM BOWERS, screenwriter

"I was a producer on *Support Your Local Sheriff*. An old friend of mine came down on the set and said, 'Well, how do you like producing?' I said, 'Oh, fine.' He said, 'What is it like?' 'See all those people?' I said. 'I'm the only one who could be hit by lightning right now and the only thing that would happen is that two weeks from now somebody would ask what happened to that guy who used to come down on the set.'"

GEORGE CUKOR, director

"A director should create a climate in which people can make fools of themselves with freedom. They have to know that there is somebody in charge. The actor has to know that you're not an ass, that if he does something extraordinarily good you will recognize it, and that you will smell out anything that's phony. Try to direct with modesty and with an open mind. Be on the level. Know what you're doing, and if you don't, don't fake it.

"I don't like a lot of talk. That is a terrible pain in the ass. Never mind what the actor thinks, what you think—just do it, in a businesslike way. When actors intellectualize and are pretentious, that is the death of everything. I respect very much the actor's instinct. I'm not terribly interested in everybody's opinion at that time.

"Very often I'm starting a scene, and much to my surprise the actor reads it in a quite different way from what I imagined, and better. Then I go with it. You cannot have a closed mind. I've never had an argument with a talented actor in my life. The only ones who kick are stupid ones. I don't mean that we don't have little awkward moments. But people say, 'How did you manage those big actresses?' Well, they are all intelligent women. In our business, women are not foolish. The director must not be scared of the actors. The actor has to know that you're looking at him sympathetically."

ALAN ALDA, actor-director

"It's a tremendous advantage to work with a director who sees and hears what you're doing. That sounds like a basic requirement, but it is not present with many directors, and with them you come up against a stone wall. If the director will only let you know that he or she has seen and heard what took place, the performance will improve tenfold, because then the actor won't try so hard to make the point and won't give you a gross version of it, but will give you the fine-tuned version."

ANTHONY QUINN, actor

"Most directors in the motion-picture business are traffic cops. I must say that out of the hundred and seventy pictures I've done, I've been directed, at the most, fifteen or sixteen times. For an actor to survive in this business, he has to learn to protect himself in the clinches. He has to learn almost to direct himself, and you can make a lot of enemies that way. My feeling about a director is that I would like to help him, but, amazingly enough, most directors don't want help. I love and adore Fellini, and would give anything to make another movie with him, but he says, 'No, no, you talk too much. I don't want you to direct my pictures, I want to direct my own pictures.'

"I don't want the director ever to be a dictator, but I expect it to be a cooperative effort. For me the ideal actor-director relationship is when a director finds a dimension of me that I've forgotten, or opens a side of me I've hidden, and says, 'Fine, trust it, trust your instincts, be as bad as you want to be.' What I expect from a director is respect, and I expect to respect him, and I expect to be given a great hand in being a creator, not just a puppet."

MARILYN BERGMAN, songwriter

"Sometimes you feel that you've not really made a contribution to a film or that what you did wasn't used properly or that maybe you shouldn't have done it all because you were superfluous. But, happily, there are other films, such as *The Happy Ending* [directed by Richard Brooks, 1971]. Richard Brooks said, 'I am writing a part for you in my movie.' When he showed us the rough cut of the film, he had indeed left big holes, allowing us to make a major contribution to particular scenes, to be an extension of the screenwriter."

DAVID WALSH, cinematographer

"I am finding that art directors are becoming more and more important to what I do. The better the art director who's working on our film, the better chance I have of making a good-looking film. People often say about films, 'Wasn't it beautifully photographed?' Well, in some cases, it really isn't beautifully photographed; it's the art direction."

CALEB DESCHANEL, cinematographer

"There are so many important people on a crew. A lot of people think the grip is a guy who just carries stuff around. But Clyde

Hart, who was the key grip on *Being There* [the film version of the Jerzy Kosinski novel, directed by Hal Ashby and starring Peter Sellers, 1979], would come up to me and say, 'Did you notice that light hitting Peter Sellers when he goes over there?' He'd be right, and we would change it. When you're shooting, you don't always notice everything. Gary Holt, the gaffer, would make suggestions about how to simplify the lighting by 50 percent, and it would be a great way of accomplishing the same thing. Craig Denault, my assistant, would come up with solutions for the rhythm of changing the focus back and forth that would be better than I would have. There's an art to the job of the dolly grip, too. When do you start the dolly? How do you start it? It's like musical orchestration how the assistant follows focus, whether it's a half note or a full note, and whether the dolly grip is allegro or pianissimo. You could use musical scores to show how a film is put together, with all the elements of the crew, the actors, and the camera."

JEROME HELLMAN, producer

"The collaboration between a producer and a director is a sensitive and subtle one under the best of circumstances. Each has a certain pride of authorship and a certain kind of creative energy. A first-rate director has a very private vision. He's selfish about it. If you push him to the wall, the truth is that he doesn't want to share that with anybody. My choice of directors has always been based first and foremost on my feeling about their work, and, second, on a lot of discussion that fundamentally satisfies me that their attitudes about the material are consonant with my own feelings.

"Directors are all different, in the way that all of us are different. Hal Ashby [for whom Hellman produced *Coming Home,* 1978] is a very different individual from John Schlesinger [for whom Hellman produced *Midnight Cowboy,* 1969, and *The Day of the Locust,* 1975]. John would think nothing of calling me on the set if he was having trouble with a scene and saying, 'Look, dear boy, I don't think this is working. Take a look at it. What do you think?' But that's not Hal's way, at least not with me. I guess just as Hal had to learn to deal with a producer who has a ferocious sense of possession and creative drives, I had to learn to deal with a director who had no reason to trust me yet on that level, and whose personality didn't necessarily lead him to trust me on that level. Accommodations had to be made on both sides, and out of that push-pull came a productive collaboration.

"There are certain common-denominator characteristics, it seems to me, that all good directors have—most of all, curiosity and an open mind. To be accessible to the unexpected. Not to go into a scene so committed to how it's going to look that you don't see something fantastic happening right in front of your eyes. I've seen directors who are blind. God help anybody who invents something; something that's ten times better than what they planned is happening on the set, and all of their energy is brought to bear to stop it, because that's not what they've planned. We've all seen their movies. That's the most important lesson."

PAUL MORRISSEY, director

"Anybody can take film. Anybody can edit film. The hard thing is to appear in front of the camera and be interesting. I don't think anybody can learn to be interesting in front of the camera. You're either interesting or you're not. That's the mysterious part of filmmaking.

"You can study directors, but you can also study the costume maker and the person who built the stars' homes. I don't think the directors make the big contributions. They help the actors make contributions that will last for hundreds of years. What makes a film stand up is the fact that Garbo was in it and John Wayne gave a great performance and Clint Eastwood shot a hundred people.

"Direction has been so overemphasized that the performer and the character have fallen into disrepute today. In *The Sugarland Express* [directed by Steven Spielberg, 1973], which wasn't a bad film, there was so much technology that you mostly remember the car. I don't think you learn much about the crazy people who were in the car, which would have been nice. Recently *Dodsworth* [directed by William Wyler, 1936] was shown at Filmex [the Los

Angeles International Film Exposition]. It's supposed to take place all over Europe, and William Wyler said afterward that he had made it all in the studio. That's the same attitude I have. I prefer letting the actors do as much as possible and not running around with the camera."

RICHARD ATTENBOROUGH, actor-director

"If you are fortunate enough as a director to cast with freedom, and you cast the best actors you can find, then it seems to me totally ludicrous when they come on the set to restrict them. In other words, to start directing them the moment they appear, to tell them precisely how the scene must be played. The chances are that if they are good at their job, and they've done their home-work, they will come up with something beyond your considera-tion. If it works and if it can be contained, you will achieve some-thing extra for which you ultimately take the credit.

"Every actor that I know is, without exception, terrified. Deep inside they are lacking in confidence. When we rehearse privately in the theater, you don't mind making a fool of your-self, you don't mind experimenting. But the moment you go on the set of a film, not only the crew are present, but there are al-ways other people on the set too. Suddenly somebody shouts 'Quiet!' and you've got to present your wares. The most impor-tant thing a director has to do at that stage is grant the artists total confidence. He must convince them that what they can offer is the best anybody could hope for. If you can manage to do that, they will relax, and if they relax, they will not play safe, and the chances are you will come up with something very exciting in-deed."

BILLY DEE WILLIAMS, actor

"I met Laurence Olivier in 1960 when I was doing the play *A Taste of Honey* with his wife, Joan Plowright. I had all of the questions prepared that I wanted to talk to this man about. He wouldn't let me ask anything. He kept asking *me* questions all the time. I said, 'Now, that's interesting. That's a sign of what a real artist is. Somebody who's probing, and listening, and wanting to know.' "

MARTIN SHEEN, actor

"If I'm playing a character who really lived, I try to find out as much about him as I can. If he has any kin who are still living, I try to contact them and talk to them without interfering with their lives too much. And then I try to be compassionate, try to fall in love with the person, no matter what he's done that you've got to portray. I try to find something in myself that is a bit akin to that. We're all capable of doing what any one person in the world has done, throughout the history of the human race. You try to find something to explore in yourself that you are proud of and something to explore in yourself that you are ashamed of, and you usually will find that it fits into any character you play."

ROMAN POLANSKI, director

"I never think of camera—not until the scene has been almost lit. I think camera is the last thing. You see, to think of the camera first is like tailoring a suit and then looking for a person who will fit it. I'd rather get the person and take the measurements and then make a suit for him."

GORDON WILLIS, cinematographer

"I never walk into a room and say to the director, 'How do you want me to light this room?' You can light it fifty ways, depending on what it is you have to accomplish. What's important for me to ask the director is, 'What is the movie about? What is it you want to say?' Once you have the philosophy of the movie, you're no longer vulnerable. If you don't know what the picture's about and what you're trying to say, you just sit there."

ALEXANDER MACKENDRICK, director and teacher

"Most directors are in a state of terror. I'm thinking of the day I started shooting my first American movie, *Sweet Smell of Success*. We started shooting in Times Square at rush hour, and we had high-powered actors and a camera crane and police help and all the rest of it, but we didn't have any script. We knew where we were going vaguely, but that's all. Nothing can be more likely to melt your bowels than that kind of absolute horror. At those moments the desperation you work from often becomes a kind of strength—there's no moment of indecision because you've got to make a decision fast, right or wrong. The director often does the best things he does under that kind of pressure, because decisions have got to be made from the subconscious."

THOMAS RICKMAN, screenwriter

"The trap most writers get into is to start thinking they know the tricks and the formulas. You say, 'If I pick a subject that hasn't been done lately, such as running, and if I write two strong male leads and a part for Liza Minnelli, then I'm going to sell this.' It may, in fact, be made. That doesn't mean it will be a good picture. The point is that the creative wellsprings have been poisoned. A lot of filmmakers are psyching out the market the way executives and lawyers and agents do, and more and more pictures are originating from executives, because the finances are so great that it's hard to get a small picture of any kind made. The quality of movies in general is declining to a very, very low point right now.

"Most of the people I know who work in films are going crazy. Trying to get films done is tough enough, but trying to get them done the way you think they should be done gets harder and harder. You really get worn down after a while fighting these battles. Most writers don't even try anymore. When you've been in the business for a while, you just take the money and run. It's practically the axiom of the Writers Guild.

"Disgruntled writers are all the same. But you're asked to

bear a lot. You're asked to allow yourself to be cut off from your work, to have no say in how your work is done. Your name is on it, all right, and you recognize the ghost of a thing you once worked on for a long time, but it's not yours. It's gotten hijacked along the way. The writer of the most miserable one-act play in New York will have more say than you will have on a $15 million movie.

"Maybe it's changing a bit now, but for so many years the critics ignored the writer altogether or deliberately downgraded the writer. That hurts. When a critic writes about something he likes about a picture and gives it to the director, and you know that you sat there one night and thought it up all by yourself, that takes its toll. A writer can be happy as long as he adjusts to the realities, knows what his job is and how far he's allowed to go."

MEL BROOKS, actor-writer-director

"I wrote *The Producers* with help from my secretary, Alpha-Betty Olsen, who works now as a comedy writer, and I went to every studio. Every studio said, 'Please. No. Try not to come back here.' Joe Levine said yes, but no to Brooks to direct. He wanted a real director. We had lunch. He hadn't read the script but he liked the idea. He liked to hear things, like the old Hollywood producers; they never read anything: 'Tell it to me,' they'd say. At the meeting, I ate very nicely; I didn't want to make any mistakes. Nothing dropped out of my mouth, I didn't eat bread and butter because I didn't know whether you should cut the bread or break it or what. Meanwhile, Joe ate like an animal. I had nothing to worry about. At the end of the meal, Levine turned to me casually and said, 'You think you can direct a picture?' I said, 'Sure.' He said, 'OK, go ahead,' and he shook my hand. He was impressed with me. He thought I was nice and cute and funny."

JOSEPH LOSEY, director

"The really creative writer contribution comes from people who write novels, plays, and poems, not just films. There is a particular breed of people in Hollywood who have never written anything but film scripts. To me, this is a horror. The idea of a screenwriter to me is an abomination. I like to work with writers who are writers."

MICHAEL CAINE, actor

"Improvisation is an extraordinary egotism. If you turn down a script that somebody has been writing for ten years and then think you can write one in your head as the camera rolls, it's a bit rough, isn't it?"

NICHOLAS RAY, director

"Improvisation has to be worked out as carefully as a three-act play."

NEIL SIMON, playwright-screenwriter

"I toyed with the idea of directing, but fortunately for me and for the world, I've given up on it. I have no affinity for directing. I don't like talking to the actors, because if I say, 'I think you ought to move over there' and they ask why, I say, 'Leave me alone, will you?' I just know it's better if they go over there."

GEORGE ROY HILL, director

"If you're head-on with the studio executives, the best thing is not to preview your film at all but go with your judgment. When I did my first film out here, *Period of Adjustment*, I had a big fight with my producer, Lawrence Weingarten, over a sequence I thought I had botched up and was embarrassed about and wanted out. He thought it was all right and necessary and he wanted it in. We went to the preview. I got up halfway through the movie to stretch my back. They were putting out tables in the lobby with preview cards, and I was seized by an inspiration. I went across the street to a drugstore and bought six different types of pencils and pens. I grabbed a handful of the preview cards, went into the manager's office, and in different hands, different phrasing, criticized that scene and stuffed the cards into the box. Larry called me a couple of days later and said, 'You know, you were right about that scene.' Since that time I have never allowed preview cards at any of my movies, because I think someone is going to try to pull the same thing on me sometime."

KING VIDOR, director

"Good wine gets better with age and bad wine gets worse with age. I think that pictures are the same way: bad pictures get worse and good pictures get better."

OLIVIA DE HAVILLAND, actress

"I never saw *The Adventures of Robin Hood* when it came out in 1938. I was afraid to see it; you are always afraid of not being any good. Fifteen or twenty years later, it was playing in Paris on the Champs Elysées, and my ten-year-old son wanted to see it. So I took him to see *Robin Hood* on a Saturday afternoon. I had no *idea* it was so good. It was enchanting. I thought, 'Good gracious, it's a classic!' When we made those films we had no idea what we were making.

"When I came home after seeing it, I sat down and wrote Errol Flynn a letter. Because I knew his particular torment over his films—he wanted to do serious work the way I did—I told him that I had just seen the film and that it was wonderful. I said, 'If you haven't seen it, go and see it as soon as you can, because I know you'll feel the same pride in having done it that I feel now.' Then I thought, 'Oh, he'll think I am sentimental,' and I put the letter in the wastepaper basket.

"Not long afterward, the phone call came, and a French journalist said, 'We have some sad news to tell you. Your partner Errol Flynn is dead.' That was one of the biggest blows I ever had. It was the end of a whole part of my life when he died."

SIDNEY SHELDON, novelist-screenwriter

"You will learn as you work in this business that any picture which is a failure hurts you deeply. When *Lost Horizon* [the 1973 musical remake of the 1937 Frank Capra classic] comes out and gets bad reviews, one day those reviews will be very expensive for you. If a studio loses money on a picture and you come in the next week with a project, you are going to find it a lot harder to get through the door. But if they have a big hit, or a lot of hits, they are in a position to make more movies. When the moviegoing public sees a picture they don't like, they are going to think ten times before they will spend money to see a picture, which could be your picture. If they go to a movie they love, then the attitude is 'Let's go see another movie next week.' That could be your movie. So never gloat about anyone else's failure, because in a very real sense it's your failure."

CAROL BURNETT, actress

"If you have faith in yourself and you have the talent, you will earn a living in this business. But don't be foolish—I wouldn't give more than five years of dedicated work going for it. This is what I was told in college, and I kept that in the back of my mind when I went to New York. Give yourself five years of not starving—I had a part-time job checking hats in a women's tearoom for $30 a week, which left me $12 a week to blow any way I wanted. You have to get that part-time job so you don't look hungry when you make the rounds and so you don't look desperate, because then you look a little mad. But after about five years, if it ain't happening, chances are that unless there's a miracle it might not."

ALEXANDER MACKENDRICK, director and teacher

"I'm more and more fascinated with the question of 'Can film-making be taught?' Quite frankly, I don't think it can. What I do think we can do is provide an environment in which it can be learned. All the kids come in straight from high school and they know they are the new Antonioni; all they need is the hardware, and then they can be one of the greatest directors ever. The main thing we do, as kindly and as gently as possible, is undermine that arrogance. We expose them to all the things they don't know and might want to learn about.

"The only thing I can promise to the youngsters I'm working with, and to you, is that as you come out and enter the industry it will be nothing like the world I knew, and maybe not even like the world is now. The thing is changing so damned fast and in such a fascinating way—not necessarily for the good—that all that can be taught is the capacity to adjust to change. In other words, all you can teach is the learning process. You can't teach the answers. You can only teach the technique of phrasing questions."

Suggested Reading

These listings include books on the seminar participants and their work, and other books of interest dealing with the general areas of filmmaking in which the participants are involved.

THE STUDIO EXECUTIVE

Adler, Richard P. (editor). *"All in the Family": A Critical Appraisal*. New York: Praeger, 1979.

Arlen, Michael J. *The View from Highway 1: Essays on Television*. New York: Farrar, Straus & Giroux, 1976.

Brown, Les. *Television: The Business Behind the Box*. New York: Harcourt Brace Jovanovich, 1971.

Cole, Barry (editor). *Television Today: A Close-Up View*. New York: Oxford University Press, 1981.

Friendly, Fred W. *Due to Circumstances Beyond Our Control*. New York: Random House, 1967.

Marsh, Spencer. *God, Man, and Archie Bunker*. New York: Harper & Row, 1975.

Marsh, Spencer. *Edith the Good*. New York: Harper & Row, 1977.

Metz, Robert. *CBS: Reflections in a Bloodshot Eye*. Chicago: Playboy Press, 1975.

Paley, William S. *As It Happened*. New York: Doubleday, 1979.

THE PRODUCER

Dunne, John Gregory. *The Studio*. New York: Farrar, Straus & Giroux, 1969.

Kanin, Garson. *Hollywood*. New York: Viking, 1974.

Korda, Michael. *Charmed Lives: A Family Romance*. New York: Random House, 1979.

Levine, Joseph. *"A Bridge Too Far": Notes from a Film Maker.* New York: Joseph E. Levine Presents, 1977.

McClintick, David. *Indecent Exposure: A True Story of Hollywood and Wall Street.* New York: Morrow, 1982.

Marx, Samuel. *Mayer and Thalberg: The Make-Believe Saints.* New York: Random House, 1975.

Selznick, David O.; edited by Rudy Behlmer. *Memo from David O. Selznick.* New York: Viking, 1972.

Thomas, Bob. *Walt Disney.* New York: Simon and Schuster, 1976.

Wallis, Hal, and Charles Higham. *Starmaker: The Autobiography of Hal Wallis.* New York: Macmillan, 1980.

THE DIRECTOR

Bazin, André; edited by François Truffaut; translated by W. W. Halsey II and William H. Simon. *Jean Renoir.* New York: Simon and Schuster, 1973.

Capra, Frank. *The Name Above the Title.* New York: Macmillan, 1971.

Renoir, Jean. *Ecrits 1926–1971.* Paris: Pierre Belford, 1974.

Renoir, Jean; translated by Norman Denny. *My Life and My Films.* New York: Atheneum, 1974.

Renoir, Jean; translated by Randolph and Dorothy Weaver. *Renoir, My Father.* Boston: Little, Brown, 1958.

Sarris, Andrew. *The American Cinema.* New York: Dutton, 1969.

Sesonske, Alexander. *Jean Renoir: The French Films 1924–1939.* Cambridge, Mass.: Harvard University Press, 1980.

Sherman, Eric (editor), for The American Film Institute. *Directing the Film: Film Directors on Their Art.* Boston: Little, Brown, 1976.

Truffaut, François, with Helen G. Scott. *Hitchcock.* New York: Simon and Schuster, 1966.

THE SCREENWRITER

Brady, John. *The Craft of the Screenwriter.* New York: Simon and Schuster, 1981.

Corliss, Richard (editor). *The Hollywood Screenwriters.* New York: Avon, 1972.

Corliss, Richard. *Talking Pictures: Screenwriters in the American Cinema, 1927–1975.* Woodstock, N.Y.: Overlook Press, 1974.

Dardis, Tom. *Some Time in the Sun.* New York: Scribners, 1976.

Froug, William. *The Screenwriter Looks at the Screenwriter.* New York: Macmillan, 1972.

Goldman, William. *Adventures in the Screen Trade: A Personal View of Hollywood and Screenwriting.* New York: Warner Books, 1983.

Hecht, Ben. *A Child of the Century.* New York: Simon and Schuster, 1954.

Karton, Joshua (editor). *Film Scenes for Actors.* New York: Bantam Books, 1983. (Contains excerpts from Robert Towne's screenplays for *Chinatown* and *Shampoo.*)

THE ACTOR

Chaplin, Charles. *My Autobiography.* New York: Simon and Schuster, 1964.

Chase, Donald (editor), for The American Film Institute. *Filmmaking: The Collaborative Art.* Boston: Little, Brown, 1975.

Cole, Toby, and Helen Krich Chinoy (editors). *Actors on Acting.* New York: Crown, 1949.

Druxman, Michael. *Charlton Heston.* New York: Pyramid, 1976.

Heston, Charlton; edited by Hollis Alpert. *The Actor's Life: Journals 1956–1976.* New York: Dutton, 1976.

Olivier, Laurence. *Confessions of an Actor: An Autobiography.* New York: Simon and Schuster, 1982.

Ross, Lillian, and Helen Ross. *The Player: A Profile of an Art.* New York: Simon and Schuster, 1962.

Rovin, Jeff. *The Films of Charlton Heston.* Secaucus, N.J.: Citadel Press, 1977.

THE ACTRESS

Brooks, Louise. *Lulu in Hollywood.* New York: Knopf, 1982.

Davis, Bette. *The Lonely Life.* New York: Putnam, 1962.

Gish, Lillian, with Ann Pinchot. *The Movies, Mr. Griffith, and Me.* Englewood Cliffs, N.J.: Prentice-Hall, 1969.
Haskell, Molly. *From Reverence to Rape: The Treatment of Women in the Movies.* New York: Holt, Rinehart and Winston, 1973.
Higham, Charles. *Bette: The Life of Bette Davis.* New York: Macmillan, 1980.
Kay, Karyn, and Gerald Peary (editors). *Women and the Cinema.* New York: Dutton, 1977.
Ringgold, Gene. *The Films of Bette Davis.* New York: Cadillac and Citadel, 1966.
Stine, Whitney, with Bette Davis. *Mother Goddam.* New York: Hawthorn, 1974.

THE CINEMATOGRAPHER

Balshofer, Fred J., and Arthur C. Miller, with the assistance of Bebe Bergsten. *One Reel a Week.* Berkeley and Los Angeles: University of California Press, 1967.
Brownlow, Kevin. *The Parade's Gone By.* New York: Knopf, 1968.
Campbell, Russell (compiler and editor). *Practical Motion Picture Photography.* Cranbury, N.J.: A. S. Barnes, 1970.
Higham, Charles. *Hollywood Cameramen: Sources of Light.* Bloomington: Indiana University Press, 1970.
Maltin, Leonard. *The Art of the Cinematographer.* New York: Dover, 1976.
Rainsberger, Todd. *James Wong Howe, Cinematographer.* Cranbury, N.J.: A. S. Barnes, 1981.
Young, Freddie, and Paul Petzold. *The Work of the Motion Picture Cameraman.* New York: Hastings House, 1972.

THE COMPOSER

Bazelon, Irwin. *Knowing the Score: Notes on Film Music.* New York: Van Nostrand, 1975.

Eisenstein, Sergei. *The Film Form*. New York: Harcourt, Brace, 1949.

Eisenstein, Sergei. *The Film Sense*. New York: Harcourt, Brace, 1947.

Evans, Mark. *Soundtrack: The Music of the Movies*. New York: Hopkinson and Blake, 1975.

Huntley, John, and Roger Manvell. *The Technique of Film Music*. New York: Hastings House, 1957 *et seq*.

Limbacher, James L. (editor). *Film Music: From Violin to Video*. Metuchen, N.J.: Scarecrow Press, 1974.

Prendergast, Roy M. *Film Music: A Neglected Art*. New York: Norton, 1977.

Thomas, Tony. *Music for the Movies*. Cranbury, N.J.: A. S. Barnes, 1973.

THE PRODUCTION DESIGNER

Barsacq, Léon; revised and edited by Elliott Stein. *Caligari's Cabinet and Other Grand Illusions: A History of Film Design*. Boston: New York Graphic Society, 1976.

Chase, Donald (editor), for The American Film Institute. *Filmmaking: The Collaborative Art*. Boston: Little, Brown, 1975.

Corliss, Mary, and Carlos Clarens (assemblers). "The Hollywood Art Director." Special section of *Film Comment* magazine, May–June 1978.

Larson, Orville K. (editor). *Scene Design for Stage and Screen*. East Lansing: Michigan State University Press, 1961.

Marner, Terence St. John. *Film Design*. Cranbury, N.J.: A. S. Barnes, 1974.

THE COSTUME DESIGNER

Benesh, Carolyn. *Reflections of Edith Head: An Exhibition of Costumes and Sketches*. Los Angeles: California Museum of Science and Industry, 1976.

Chierichietti, David. *Hollywood Costume Design*. New York: Harmony Books, 1976.

Head, Edith, and Jane Kesner Ardmore. *The Dress Doctor*. Boston: Little, Brown, 1959.

Head, Edith, with Joe Hyams, illustrated by Edith Head. *How to Dress for Success*. New York: Random House, 1967.

McConathy, Dale, with Diana Vreeland. *Hollywood Costume*. New York: Harry N. Abrams in cooperation with the Metropolitan Museum of Art, 1976.

THE CASTING DIRECTOR

Blanchard, Nina. *How to Break into Motion Pictures, Television, Commercials and Modeling*. New York: Doubleday, 1978.

Selznick, Joyce. *Blue Roses*. New York: Bantam, 1980.

Shurtleff, Michael. *Audition*. New York: Walker, 1978.

THE INDEPENDENT FILMMAKER

Brakhage, Stan; edited by Robert A. Haller. *Brakhage Scrapbook: Collected Writings 1964–1980*. New Paltz, N.Y.: Documentext, 1982.

Brakhage, Stan. *Film Biographies*. Berkeley, Calif.: Turtle Island, 1977.

Brakhage, Stan. "Metaphors on Vision." Special issue of *Film Culture* magazine, Autumn 1963.

Clark, Dan. *Brakhage*. New York: Film-Makers Cinematheque Monograph Service, 1966.

Lipton, Lenny. *Independent Filmmaking*. San Francisco: Straight Arrow, 1972.

Renan, Sheldon. *An Introduction to the American Underground Film*. New York: Dutton, 1967.

Ritchie, Donald. *Stan Brakhage—A Retrospective*. New York: The Museum of Modern Art, 1970.

Sitney, P. Adams. *Visionary Film*. New York: Oxford University Press, 1974.

Index

227

About the Editor

Joseph McBride is an author and screenwriter whose scripts include the cult classic *Rock 'n' Roll High School* and several television specials, including the American Film Institute Life Achievement Award tributes to James Stewart, Fred Astaire, Frank Capra, and John Huston, for which he has received an Emmy nomination and three Writers Guild of America Awards nominations. He has written or edited twelve other books, including *John Ford, Orson Welles, Hawks on Hawks,* and *High & Inside: The Complete Guide to Baseball Slang.* He was formerly business editor and film critic for *Variety* and *Daily Variety.*